SUSAN BLANSHARD

SHEET STONE

PAGE ADDIE PRESS
UNITED KINGDOM. AUSTRALIA

Sheetstone: /Susan Blanshard Copyright©2024.Third Edition. ISBN: 978-1-916709-23-2 is published by Page-Addie Press, United Kingdom. 1. Poetry, English. 2. Travellers- Poetry. 1.Title. First Edition Spuyten Duyvil, New York City. ISBN 978-933132-12-9 All rights reserved. No reproduction, copy or transmission of this Publication may be made without written permission from the author. No paragraph of this publication may be reproduced, copied or transmitted. Save with written permission or in accordance with provisions of the Copyright, Designs and Patents Act 1988, or under the terms of any license permitting limited copying, issued by the Copyright Licensing Agency. The Author has asserted his right to be identified as the author of this work in accordance with the Copyright, Design and Patents Act 1988.

CONTENTS

PART 1	5
DIALOGUE OF DESIRE	
POEM OF THE INTIMATE	6
OPIUM	8
FRAGMENTS	12
BONE AND RIVER	14
INTIMATE ROOMS	16
SILK	19
PILLOW SPEAK	21
MEMOIR FOR A LOVER	27
THE ARTIST AT MOUNT VICTORIA	28
SEX/FLESH/SPIRIT	32
THE ESSAYS	32
PART II	44
DIALOGUE OF THE INTIMATE	
PLACES SHE RETURNS TO WITH EYES CLOSED	47
PART III	52
THE ART OF LOVE	
UNIVERSAL QUESTIONS	60
PART IV	62
THE ARTICLES OF EXPOSURE	
PART V	68
FRAGMENTARY THOUGHTS	
PAINTED CHRONICLES	77
UNIVERSAL QUESTIONS 2/2	80
MONOLITHIC	86
UNIVERSAL QUESTIONS 3/3	92
THE MUSEUM OF SMALL FINDINGS	98
THE FUGITIVE TEARS	104
DECEMBER	107
FEBRUARY	108
MARCH	112
TWO HUMAN ERRORS	116
A LINE DRAWN THROUGH MID-POINT ON A CIRCLE	117
CONVERSATIONS BEFORE LEAVING	121
FOSSILS OF US	128

PART 1

DIALOGUE OF DESIRE

POEM OF THE INTIMATE

In this bed
we hold together
and when we speak
our words drifted on this
beach of fallen water.

Blind before
our eyes returned
as the constant river
holding us
in the physical world
the song of us
the falling of eyelids before
sleep.

Holding shadows in your fingers
inside the conception
behind the emotion
and the way your hair
falls across my face
like soft shadow

inside my desire
and the orgasm
between the sex
and the way
the binding
tightens the drum
of my skin.

You are musk, the smell
of a woman fills your room
slow suck of earth
the way you
enter me

the seed in the core
the message in code
the way we exist before
we were lovers.

OPIUM

All night is within us.

I will say our secret... of sex & love, this drug
of dream & surrender.

Speak now of the inner image, a vein
of warm inside us, of a burnished leaf rubbed on
the outer image of my skin. Black edge where the
leaf fell and touched the ground. The willow of
us, the seed and flame of desire. For only fire will
hear us.

This is the grace of remembered things, charcoal
on your fingers organic heat of the long bone.
Some said you were a disciple. Others said you
were sacred. I likened you to a spell you place me
under. Honey to your woman.

Your sex is a drug. Orgasm is opium.

And I love your musk, as it drifts over your body
and it fills my mind like incense.

Your musk is a drug. Orgasm is opium.

And I love to feel your lips as they kiss my mouth
tasting pith and sex stone. Imprint of your lips. A
man who kisses like fire summons my soul back.

And I love to feel your moisture. Like a cool
bath in the desert. Atonement in the sand crossed

between birth and dying. Pale stains of rust and
undatable dust. Divine seam where all love ends.
And begins again.

Sex in the long hours, I feel desire in our time,
the bread and wine. Rapture of skin. The rooms
we slept in & lay bare in.

Your robe held the shape of your body with desire
in folds, draped anthropomorphic over chair. Six
o'clock. I enter your room. It is warm in there.

Naked, we move through a thousand furnished
rooms. You placed a quilt on the bed; we lay
to love, in crewel culpa of birds, wings of
wool, dusky velvets embroidered with parrots
(hovering) between (reality).

And the silk flowed down between and it is the
weight of your hand pressed in the small of my
back that arouses me. A moment, I tell myself,
which you have given to me.

Lying in the bed, where most of our riches are,
dreamed, imagined. You could hear the poetry of
rain as the thatch-cutter patterning the sky above
us. As if the clouds understand. While we sleep. I
dream of no other lover.

A dream fastened across shadows that fade behind
the city facade. Or deadened in mornings traffic.
The rush hour on harbor bridge. In a dreams
binding wishes, of infinite unconsciousness,
thought for the dreamer, his sleeping eyelids
closing.

Summer...dissolves the ceilings of days held in

doubled incantations dissolve the light. And I can see part of your shadow, near the peach tree, its closeness and separations. And there is a blue deck chair, a path, crows on the grass, or black shoes.

Through a tiny aperture of peach leaf & black skin grape, clicking the film of memory as a wasp buzzes in vine & time, past noon, the day embalmed in wasp & cicada song. A memento towards shell of sun, with you on the bench, in the hours, you see the cotton of his shirt is faded, and stained with peach, closer still and you detect the taste of nectar on his lips.

Close your eyes.

Now you see yourself.

What pulls us closer?

Sex?

Opiate wand.

The drug of us.

At the still point of the warm moon, I saw long light in your eyes. Echo in your face, I saw, your jawbone fixed like the slant of the air when you saw me watching you, and then your smile broke into an arc of love with your lips. The smile was familiar to me. Then he smiled again.

I can see everything you do. But I know no more than you, the Lover said.

The split of two when the shell cracked, as if
we could touch surrender between us: pulse and
sweat beating on silk of throat triangle, secret
whispers of us tangled in a night. I stay embraced
in the forearms of a Lover holding me. I feel the
warm rush, through layer and layer, erotic earth, I
soaked it up, the love sensual and lucent my wet
finger vanilla or mossy balm sweetest taste of
syrup, ripening plum and untranslatable feeling as
I put it in my mouth.

It is harder to define these tender ghosts. Sweet
juices of intimacy: the Lover said.

Thick smell of the honey room. The rhyme is
also yours to enter the palace of bees and find
the sweetest honey in the body of love, knowing
the secret, the nights, mornings, afternoons, the
rooms as close as this is, having filled a moment
with its own pollen, I discovered a lifelong taste
for this divine recipe, entering my mouth, liquid
languish of the ancient, as close as getting to
this, slipping your tongue into the closest part,
knowing the secret feel of you, I need no longer
dream it.

FRAGMENTS

A few pages lightly stained with a virtually undetectable paper (flaw). Dust, ashes, sand, gritty boundaries can be read like an elegant text for the initiated. The paper flaw touching the final line of text. Reads: to be grateful for fragments leftover, the remains, smaller than small.
I find these fragments since you invited me in. Not invited, so to speak. In opening the door and entering, in this brief passage where the dreams cross over. The dream-crossed space before falling in love with you.

There was whiteness in the month: of ice paper celandine— first flower seen in March after the winter thaw. Others have loved you and have fallen through, discarded when you left them, face pressed against the window. Writing a poem in breath fog, rusted with nostalgia. They loved you too much or not enough.

How do you love another?

There are rules, he said, looking me in the eyes. To love you must first open your heart. You need to feel more for the other person than your own self. The essential thing is to enter love deeply (kiss no other lips interim, for you will taste a foreigner).

Close the door behind you...

Seen through the keyhole, candles burning in a
séance, saffron walls embalming us in firelight,
lying there, I am able to translate your warm
hands, taffeta emollient façade marks a tryst
hidden, almost forbidden.

I am held in sweet heat, immaculate tourniquet, I
am bound by it. As it tightens and transforms the
naked man in my arms, made powerful by sinews,
muscle, blood and skin, love moves into a new
space, like paths of stars, it goes on forever. And
stay in love, long enough, until it is familiar to
you as a room.

This then, my Lover is yours...

BONE AND RIVERS

A few leaves jangling in their intactness
with tiny rust holes costing a few letters.
Burning wild grasses & wallflower
brushed on the walls
and you in my room.
I have a match. No lighter.

Your kiss was a flame, on my lips carried by
physical incantation. Whose kiss now passes
surrendering through endless warmth burns,
stroking by heated stroke, ringed by your clasp
circling made my blood burn and flows with your
saliva as sweet warm lava flowing rock, every
hard stone held, every release, unreal. A woman
pulls her long dark hair and ties tight. Blindfolded
destinies. This complete seduction.

And volcanic heart beats as drum in veins our
blood is magma of the heart. I only know this
secret of fire sacrament between. And tomorrow,
who knows when the fire returns emptied ashes,
reminiscent winds that will blow the air and
our voices back together. Like incantations and
warmed waves. In this breathing in, among the
breathing out.

I will find you; the wind is blowing through our
infinite existence, pushes souls together. Side
by side. You hold me, then stand away. I want
to feel your body warmth from a distance. By
this warmth and only this, we have existence.

And when I traveled with you, I traveled with
fire. Aflame or ablaze, by love which belongs
to us. Places out of the map. Whole segments
connecting one of us to the other. Where I want
to be found on this pathway as the one traveled.
All the doorways leading to memories or through
windows shuttered in the cool breezes in our
empty rooms.

Can I step over, move the sliding door?

......as I found the key once and unlocked the
door once, move deeper into the room, I know
the room, all of our chambers, thinking of the
dwelling, light in each archway. I lay beside
you, like a dream-teller, speaking to your very
existence, each breath folding in and out of your
lungs, a heart beating, repeating perfectly, caged
by bones (his whole life) repetitions in circadian
& primordial rhythm. Traversed by your body
span, part muscle, part sinew. Strong steel of a
man in the night. Like iron ore vice: hold me
tight. Into the pulse, the moving and breathing,
subtle like a shape of forged or softly welded
parts. I want to be filled with you, sinew, muscle,
bone; nothing breaks the feeling of you. Bone and
river poem rediscovered here.

INTIMATE ROOMS

*I do not hope that this man will escape sex &
love, this drug of dream ivory surrender in the
opiate room.*

And all this time, I have shared your room as if I
am the only woman. I came here on my own and
have been sleeping there under your earth. And
room by room, touch by touch. Earth smells of
aftershave anointment, all the things you touched
with your hands, and moss you left with all the
bedroom musk, as it exists with all the night.

Feelings go beyond, and the rush inside going
back to first time, where the white sheets
laundered with sunlight, over summer. Pith of
interlude and white sheets crumpled by this
biology, this intimate theology. What divine
things we do in this sacred prayer. I sat on your
bed, waiting, with a silver plate almonds & wine.
The Holy fragment beyond understanding.

What images return? The old villa built between
a fish shop and a tattoo parlor. Faded paint and
cracked windows. The images trailing through the
doorways. Appearing and disappearing, images
transferred among the fish and ink.

Our room as a cave at night, a tent in sunlight,
a Baroque pavilion late afternoon. The intimate
shadows in the curtains ravine, red silk inflaming.
Looking at you, the moment's surrender, I can see

you... softly denuded exact shaping of shadow.
Following every curve of you. Of you and only
you, the Lover said.

It has always been this way between us. In the
semi-dark rooms, we know each other naked.
Scars, each scratch: sensing tiny perfections of
your skin where you hurt yourself once. A haze of
blood, a piece of pain. Each pigment, each tattoo,
each bruise a moving scar, an accumulation, as if
you never heal.

I want to discover the origins of you. Touch the
scars. One lifetime casts us memory, you and I
...how long had I been with you? How long—I
think. Since a winter in May at six o'clock.
Description of moments surrendered before us.
Into your arms, my arms, my body—one falls into
another.

In my heart's mind, there is no abacus to count
these moments. It isn't just days of light but these
images of interwoven things, an image of your
hair on the pillow falling over your eyes as you
turn your head, turn of your face, opening your
mouth, as if the body gives up the secret of its
stones. Like the first time you spoke my name.
(No). It felt like your voice broke my name,
breaking it open, like an ancient seal.

Warmth of the stone enter your body lower
yourself into the spring as into some liquid place
of your body's other life in sleep. Love is not
outside us, nor entirely inside but flows back and
forth between us and objects we have made the
landscape we have shaped and move in. We have
dreamed these things in our deepest lives and they

are ourselves.

The memory comes of how it was, slipping like
an envelope of afternoon sun, under the door.
Smells of sweet rain in the wet season, drumming
the earth, through scented gardens of earth and
sky. The sensual smells in the shuttered room
and mango on the plate juice on your tongue as
if summer wine, after we have sipped it, remains.
As grapes crushing into wine, in basement cellars.

And along old neighborhoods, remain the shape
of cats and our house. I feel this desire for brick,
clay, of doorways familiarity, or rusted garden
gates. But it is wooden waves of storm memory
throws at me. I am aware of the vanities of
buildings, the damp soul of concrete.

Still, you take familiarity for permanence, the
Lover whispered. It is hard to renounce the
dreams I knew for nails and planks of new
imaginary thoughts. What then?

All we have is this moment.

SILK

He stroked his hand across my cheek. His fingers brush my throat. Then warm tongue. We carry intimate ceremony, into each other.

The whole room has been transformed by memory. As if repainted, refurnished and reconstructed from my original memories. I remembered the melon walls ripe and warm with the stems of church candles burning. The white sheet dyed lime green and hung like a single curtain of fresh thought. Bits of old furniture came back, the whore's red mattress supported on four perfect columns of demolition yard bricks.

In the distance, music from wooden flute and single stringed instrument, the body made from the hard rind of a cucumber and haunting notes through a bamboo stem attached to one end of a small box. Sweet tension on a string. A flute woman playing.

We slept on her bed and her room became our room. A robe found in the second-hand store, black & white silk snapshot of embroidered birds. It was worn and faded. And I slipped my arms through a sheath of oriental sleeve. I thought of the woman who wore it before me, what created the small stain that looked like ink, a tiny stain that disappeared and reappeared in different places.

Was it the perfume she wore, designed to
make men remember her. I felt as if some of
her fragrance had spilt over me, a sweet smell
lingers there, like musk held in dust and air. Like
the room where we first made love in, keeps
returning, the long afternoons with moments of
bright or fading light casting shadows on the
walls and ceiling, dividing my thoughts between
what was and now is. The morning following.
Yes, I found it again. These thoughts slip out
easily, like my arms from the robe when I undress
in front of you.

And at the river's bend, I was looking at where
the water ends, at simple things: small rain
pavilion of your tanned skin as you dry off after
the shower, white towel, tile floor. Then your
smile, watching me watching you—as desire
expressed on a face. Your smile broke into an arc
of love with your lips.

No one asks me to confess to you, the door
opened and another man enters but I could not
kiss him. No silk red lips parting & opening
together. No breath breathing lambent into me.
Where did he go? Into another dream in this
aquarium world of damp sheets & sleep. These
nocturnal imaginings pressed against your skin.
In which the skin registers illicit shadow as a
degree of black, as carnival of night. You speak as
if you let a stranger in, kissed his lips warm and
new, you reached the part pressed into you until
you shivered, remembering the shift of earth,
but as if you read my mind, you said: I knew a
dreamers kiss has no weight to mark a tryst.

PILLOW SPEAK

*Torn into the headline, with clean tears at the
bottom margin into the final lines of text...Blood.
Lace. Some adulterated. Sheath of fire & desire.
All are censored by Saints.*

How do you know of the journey of my soul?

Each soul holding its own weight. I have seen
souls pass by like ten million golden comets
across the inky sky of heavens blue vault, seeing
Soul as red fire, nearer than stars and closer than
my eye looking upon your face.
Syrup spread like a glistening sheet held down
by milky pebbles at the edge. We lie down on the
horizon, horizontal in a place familiar. You can
hear the late night news through the apartment
wall. And we talk about the past and years beyond
this. What do you see under the curves of your
eyes?

The ascension to heavens, the heat striking white
cell inlets. You just have to define heaven with a
look, so I leave descriptions to the diarist among
us, he said.

What have we created in the world?

Nothing but love.

I have no possession to give you except myself.

There is no getting closer than this.

What am I to you?

You are the language of desire, carved on my lips. As fire. Your red mouth painted in the secret ways of sex. Our private lessons. By your pillow and the way you hair falls across my face, by your fingers as they travel the stones of my spine, I forget distance between. In his hands, he holds nothing but a small book. I will spread it out on the earth and the words will be wild flowers in the dirt. The syllables dusted with sun & grass. Warm, wet, gasp.

What do you see?

Your face locked in my memory.

Our unborn children held in your bended arm.

The room of us. This refuge forever.

I studied this passion with you, tasting it too: What is delicate and fragile. We shared sweet segments of mandarin, a child, a warm pool to bathe her in. I think about her, that distant girl, the childhood's honeycomb, bee smell of her hair. Pushing on the corners... looking at birth's potency, sweetest folium.

The garden to the songs of our past. The grass & sun. A garden of spirit and air, our life was rhyming like the song. What is beyond this?

Whatever you hear.

I hear ghosts. I heard them shout.

The last breath of the breath.

The difference between, is the breath you hold.

And with that thought, I got up from the bed and closed the window.

Thoughts painted through my mind. Knowing I loved you so much. This desire & fear like needle in the vein. Sometimes I wonder.
Is this the man who lies always beside me? I am powerless to say. When I see, there is only you and I together (knowing one of us will vanish between a heartbeat) at what point will loving you begin again?

What if I look into a room, and when you sleep, there is always another woman lying on the other side of you, her dark hair, tight and plaited. I cannot tell if you love her or will love her. And a kiss, if it is kiss marks you. When the tongue slips. And more than this. And kiss. A woman. Love bite on her throat. Taste a mouthful like biting peach. That habit you found with me holds something different for her. In a mouth.

If there were you and the woman only. Not the bed where I am sleeping in the continuous moment. But kiss of another when I go where the ghost-angel lives in the white sky. Listen to me.

Do you hear anyone else in this room?

I looked in your direction. Bare chest. Copper skin. Two pairs of bare legs entwined, our bodies

mold into a curve of shoreline. These naked
envoys, the closeness of desire.

Anyone else?

Then I answered his question. Not in this room.
It was easy lying there with him in a room away
from the street. I could feel the edges of us
sweetly embalmed the corners of the room, yes,
I understand everything, a handful of blue days
on the horizon to follow, your words held in
place and sometimes I stay a moment longer just
to hear the timbre of your voice. I am no dream
interpreter, but there is no other, the Lover said.
I smile and wonder if each word is true. And just
then, I swallow the tinctures of words, grains of
pain & laudanum of love, the feelings all over
again.

Somewhere in margins: I will feel absence, the
heat of him, night of interplay, beneath the moons
ashes there are snow fields like white rice winter,
the fields we walk through leave deep blue prints
of your feet. There is no other way to get you
out of my mind, but the thawing snows erasure.
When will the melting snow end? How long will
the winter day wait. I stand for a long time. In a
white field, near a river.

*When we scoop snow from the well. Under snow
is water.*

What will be, will be.

I want you to tell me what you have not told
anyone. What they found in the heart of the soil,
on their bones and skull, is held like a nearly

perfect embroidered secret. Did you see her?

The still one, I gazed on her face, as if she were a rock or a mountain, cold blue, still & quiet in the absence of breathing in the fog.

Where is she?

The more I wanted to see her, the less I could look. Those whose breath will break in white of noun unspoken, meaning sleep. She could stay for me no longer, saying my name. Abandoning her face, I could hear in the smallest cracking, and neither the Still One or I could not do anything stopping that fact. Those whose aura will then linger, in the basement, strange silence, visible pulse that vanishes and unbleached calico, also, a moment ago. Was it the quill or the skeletal wiring of her wings breaking through? A shroud sound, beyond the linen.

Those who return. If it's true, I have no explanations rudimentary evolution of the angels, or mystery measures of celestial passage. I now know you secrets. As sound as it pulls past linen threads. I know you, as changing light and voices. As sound aired siren or dog bark, wind banging window sash, breeze moving leaves, the drumming of moist beads, rain on the earth.

Those who slip through with transient shadow incarnations. Fainting between shadows, the pulse at your wrist fainter and fainter, fading or dying? More faded than lost and nearer to the body than I know. Leaving fragmented days of an existing sleep, living white existence, in the silence of light in this exquisite fault line. And this force has made atmosphere a destination. For this, our wings grow intimate.

I will show you her words in a handful of dust. Her first mark as a ghost. Tell her I hear the vaporous vibrations as a sound, rising to lips of stone. As she wipes her mouth with her palm. And I understand no other transparencies, no psalm or lullaby melancholy blended but voices, so close to me, standing, listening still until your soft breathing resumed.

MEMOIR FOR A LOVER

All I see is the essence of us
I saw the lover and the loved
observer and observed,
one does not teach the other this.

I fully realized,
this truth that the other speaks
aflame or ablaze this is by love,
which belongs to us.

Something more, she said
of things unknown, that leads us
to more
as you seduce another
to love.

The mystery was accomplished
illuminated by the diffusion of light
perfected by love
impregnated with memory,
I was here.

Of all we know, nothing would be
unknown.
The touch of an eyelid closing.
This could not have been seen before.

THE ARTIST AT MOUNT VICTORIA

He sleeps in a room of a disused brothel—a room with no curtains, only harlequin colored glass in the window, so no one can see inside. And the sheets on the bed, street light moon dyed, amber light against his bare skin.

Winter. All the rooms in the house are cold. The old villa marooned against the shadow of an urban mountain. Southerly wind, uninvited, pushes its way under his door, towards him and sends the cold across the floor so it can take the warmth from his tanned body, steal white heat from his bones. Each night he builds a fire in the grate using grenades of brown pine cones and crumpled drawings, then the hot fire fingers touching charcoal sketches of naked women, as fire burns.

He is alone, except inside his dreams. In one dream, there is a woman standing by a horse in a river. She does not speak to him and he wishes she would stay with him, until he wakes. But she never does. When a man finds the same woman inside dreams, he looks for her when he wakes. He pulls a small blue folder from his pocket and rolls a cigarette, thin white tissue with a trace of glue.

As the artist draws her lips, he feels he is drawing the most beautiful part of her, crimson pencil

softly feathering the creases of her smile, tracing
plump moist flesh before he kisses her. Her lips
are naked, with no lipstick wax to melt in body
heat. Unadulterated—and he wonders if he is the
first, if there has been no one else. As he detects
the taste of violet on her tongue, he knew he
counted, as the smallest grain of balance.

SHE IS SEVENTEEN.

The morning, the girl stood and watched her
clothing floating down to earth from the third
floor window. When the screaming woman dumps
all the girl's clothes, she slams the window. She
slammed the glass and frame of childhood, in the
city of earthquakes, the foundations of the house
shook again on eternal fault line, as if maternal
love was non returnable, instability felt in rooms,
in the damp basement, under Pacific Ocean to
faraway mountains, to another atmosphere.
The morning, a girl leaves home.

THE GIRL ENTERS THE BROTHEL.

Enter the front door, just one long hallway of
floral carpet worn in parts. The corridor is dimly
light. But in pale candescence, you see twelve
doors; each door leads into a double bedroom.
From the kitchen, a bathroom with twelve white
tiled showers. She looks at her reflection in the
mirror, a virgin living with the ghosts of whores
now. One shower for each whore. Many men for
each whore.

She turns the light out and lies on her back
thinking about the man in the next room. The
young artist rents a room down the hallway from

mine. When I spoke to him lightly in the kitchen, he left me with a sudden desire for him to touch me. What holds us at quiet gunpoint...how delicate, fragile the celebrations are.

Later, I hear his music coming through the bedroom wall. And the voice of a man singing lyrics about a woman of the harbor. Honey & oranges, sunshine & salvation, his fingers undressing her. One hand pushing down on delicate fret, his fingers pause on the strings. Then the chorus starts again.

Rivers are roads that move, they carry us where we want to go. Between us and heaven & hell there is only love & sex. This is what the girl believes. One evening I leave my room and enter his life without knocking. We are slaves and masters of our own acts. When I open the door, he is waiting for me.

This template of beginnings. We will share a bathtub and a child. Summa Contra Gentiles. One does not teach the other this. In memory there remains a spark that connects you back to a place, a room, perfume of white flowers, the odor of rain falling on hot pavement, ...another human being. The smallest feeling and your eye is drawn to an image. We make love on an iron bed. By the passions of my body, of carnal desires, according to my own passions, as desiring. Later you cook me crepes in a tiny cast iron pan, drizzle thyme honey over one, orange on the other.

Sunday morning, something about the way sunlight poured through a hundred panes of glass, oatmeal in blue china bowl, muscatel raisins

sticky in cream. There are bowers of pigeons
in the woods, the hum of wasps in the fig tree
outside the kitchen door. Fallen figs sticky on my
shoes.

Monday morning—pancakes again. Life as divine
recipe. And then you found a brass nutcracker.
It was shaped like a relic and then you placed an
almond and squeezed together until the shell split.
We kept the nutcracker for ourselves.

You keep this woman to yourself. You drew my
body with your charcoal, You draw me closer.
There is no other. Now the scent of almond
blossom reminds me of you. The beautiful voice
returns. Now you understand my feelings, you
feel my hand reach across to touch what I have to
give you.

You were smiling the day we signed on as
pilgrims. And then I traveled with him. I traveled
with fire. Aflame or ablaze, by love which
belongs to us. Warm ash left in the fireplace. A
clue that we slept here last night.

SEX/FLESH/SPIRIT

THE ESSAYS

I will say our secret...

we never left each other.

Before this moment, we lived together...
before there were seas we strung pearls
before grapes were crushed, we poured wine
before stars were diamonds
chipped from a reef of sky, I wore your ring.

And I carried our child on my hip
your honey in my blood.

I can't say precisely what I came for
but I felt it happening,
how we love each other in essence
by accident...

I never want to steal the smile from your lips
sculpture sadness in your eyes.
I came here by myself but I can't leave that way.
Someone else will take me home.

I want to be filled with you, skin, muscle,
bone.
photograph you inside the window frame
eyes of the shutter
half closed

a room full of sun as it breaks into rainbows
through glass
warm fragments splintered through your hair,

You are wearing the same faded shirt,
blue of Saints
found in illuminated manuscripts.

In old books, they do not save
the image of every man
but every man is worth saving.

From a distance, I believe
all men are the anointed ones.

A man's scent full pheromone, intimacy seams—
musk leather herb
primal arousal for your woman.
in a room full of
sexual hunting fertility
lover.

There were twelve male dancers,
six deer, a horse, another
man dressed as a girl, two boys,
one with a triangle
and a crossbow.

When we stop dancing, I can not
tear myself away
from your open shirt.

The woman collects blue corn flowers
in the sun.
A field of blue
her blue saturates your fabric
like a cool shower.

What were you thinking about just then?

The photographs I took of you.

Images of a young woman's body.
Hair to her waist.
Standing in a doorway, you were

naked, looking away.
Another print of you lying almost naked
a batik across your belly,
secret folded up in silence
tangerine stripes with lime.
A marble landing
on saltwater blue
of frozen sea.

You tie up a scarf
hair a bundle of warm wheat,
grain in sunlight.
the weight of light
falling off her right shoulder.
All the men wanted to touch.
An image rubbing against an image
and the other girl bending over
eyes looking into his eyes.
Rocks of her spine,
the land belongs to the past.

***

All images are dreamed first.
Slow, blue, light.
The touch of an eyelid closing.
And a timbre boy lying on gravel, watching her
change.

When the young girl disappears, a woman moves
forward.

The man recognizes her leaf
and curve, storm code composer,
holy canticle, bondage of heat.
Her words pull you to bed
and you hold her like a paper kite...the flow of

rich blood rivers.
Blind
strings of your existence on the fulcrum
of the world.

In the darkroom with the door closed

the same woman, bending over in the next print
eyes looking into his eyes.
A double look from lover to lover.

Who were you with, before we met?

I was with a girl.

An image within me. We were standing
with a saint on a bridge
when he took our
photograph.
An air full of marble dust.
He had cut through the chapel walls
when he was walking
inside my dream.

But when I woke from sleep
emptiness was in my bed.

Can I step over, move the sliding door?

I want to discover the origins of you. Touch
the scars.

Pass through your fingers like a bead of rosary.

Hold the door open for me.

How do you enter?

Move deeper into the room.
Lie down in a double bed.

Where do taste and smell begin ...

Watered blueprint
map of memory

the bones of my spine,
a divining rod.

*I fell into your life like an angel
an angel with strings
I fell through the Genesis hedge and topiary fig
into your walled garden.*

I made up my mind
to love you to the end, but then...the sky
is filled with clouds that break the skin of sky,
they float as blue strata with random lamb clouds
leading up glacier mountains.

Rain falls without a plan,
dreams & voices in the sky are unexpected
seagulls & clouds just happen...
I came here in order to love you,
one kiss, one touch, one night at a time.

I entered the whore's room and wait
while you render
a pencil drawing.
Charcoal shadows between fir trees,
open skiff filled with fish,
yards of fine-toothed netting.

A baby blanket of silk and camel hair
folded in a woman's lap; she is bending
over the side of the open boat, you draw her
scooping silver fish from the river
with her right hand open.

She has long fingers, as if she plays the organ.
A resonating box with strings of different
thickness,

the same deep note

when exposed to wind, strings rising and

falling.

Deep rolling world

in the drawing she can run over a field of wheat
without bending a single
blade.

Where is the whore?
She lap dances in stilettos and lace.
Can you hear her breathing?

The finite difference between life and a ghost is
breath
The last breath you hold for eternity.

I heard my breath.
And the seagull was waiting.
His baby feathers
gone,
he was printed grainy black and white
The scrim of him

watching me like he used too.

What astronomic path did you take to get back home?
Looking up, I saw feather tracings,
a circle drawn in morning sky.

Where is the whore?
In the room.

The room lined with yellowing paper,
iodized underlining fruits, red cardinals,
tigers with needle teeth and twisted vines of
mandrake copulating roots entering her raw pulp,
the whore's paper peeling in leafy exfoliation.

Her mouth touching paper shadows
she grazes his lips
taste sweet almond.

Her body painted with sex
nude silk rope
red candles stolen from church alter,
torch light flickers shadows on walls high ceiling
molding. St Elmo's fire playing around
makes you smile and look up.

You are wearing white sarong, gossamer
transparency,
later, you invite me into your bath.
Some baptism: delicious delirium with your body.

You are handsome
but am I too shy to be naked with you?

When I enter this place, how will I find you?

There are two fish, sweet-lipped saltwater,
swimming blue
tattoo as tide mark on my thigh.
An identifying mark is a symbol
that never changes.

You speak like a boy longing
to be a whale.

Some nights a fish metamorphous.
Buoyant waves lifting his arms
A man swims free in dreams
a brush of indigo, orchids shadows
like birds imagine,
a face on a wave behind him
but always a blue sky returns bringing
morning tinted salt
flying fish caught in transparent net.

Your bath, still warm.

Catch wind in a net, water in sieve,
silken taut moiré.
A woman is the muslin
through which my emotion strains.

Words and letters etched into phone box
glass. Speaking to me, cicadas and
clay lions crouched above on pagoda roof.
You notice the shine on the glazed tiles.

I'll be home soon: the Lover said.

You do not leave...someone lets you go: she
whispered.

What part of you will change?

A man is a hunter. He draws blood with his blade.
An artist paints in ash left by soul of the hunter.
I will paint you over time
Always your wild hair and green eyes.

What do you dream?

I always dream of a woman with green eyes.

I had been looking at the sun, but this was no accidental
color.

She was standing beside Appalachian horse
in a river when
she looked up.
There were fence posts rubbed silk by his flanks
animal shadows hardened on the banks,
in the granite rock there were impressions of hoof
prints.
It was a horse that brought you down to earth
he told me later.

As a younger girl what do you believe in?
Luck piling up and doves
shaken from silk scarves
by the magician.
Shadow boxing your wall,
enough to make you smile
and look up.

She pulls on night's shirt: dark robe of celestial
fabric, someone painted stars before she was
born, tore animal patterns from mulberry paper,
theatrical shapes etched in a far piece of earth.
When wheat fields flattened and mistral breath
spoke to her in the womb, she was sleeping in

the uterine shed, sentient being she knew she
was, albumin in blood and placental jellyfish, the
curve of her bare shoulder by which we map earth
contours; call her heroic, stalked, hunted, when
she gives, she gives by her own laws...
a woman's body is a labyrinth some men get lost
in body inking, carnal printing ...
red cherries and he kissed her, stones in her
mouth,
how he embroiders her name with his tongue.

The way I travel with you on the silk road...
through the gate, a man enters
he opens out the shutter
breaks free the rusted leaves
pull your wrist through broken window
I will stem the flow
but if you leave me now, my shadow will follow.

I am voyeur in your landscape,
I knock on your door.
dusky plums, dark coffee.
The room is a garden of ginger and opium
there are wild roses on my lips, passion
flowers, sticky resin of buds.
musk between your fingers from places
hidden

when a woman opens out
into the world.
her perfume whispers everything.

You kissed me all those years ago. What was it
you wanted from me back then?
Your body under Baroque quilt embroidered
thread, trail of tendrils and frayed oak

leaves.

Original feelings of our beginnings beneath
crewel
branches; embroidered birds of paradise fly and
Chinese figures stand guard outside
lemonwood pagodas.

A room full of private musk

the night rain has thinned out.

PART II

DIALOGUE OF THE INTIMATE

Erotic encomium of cardamom. Spices make
a woman taste, the way you like.

His tongue in her cinnamon room.

A man takes inventory
a woman's culinary
compendium.
Rough cinnamon. Tarry vanilla pod.

She grows kaffir in her garden.
A crush of lime
Sublime.

Your perfume reaches a man's most primitive
kiss on a throat.
A woman of orchard
camphire with spikenard
saffron;
calamus and cinnamon,
trees of ice pear and winter plum.

No rosary of apples: I tell you. An apple is not
a woman's temptation.
Remember...a woman took the fruit of the tree
in the midst
of the garden.

It was purple passion growing aromatic on vines

I watched you: he said

The way you tear fruit with your teeth, warm
seeds in a
mouth and then you
swallow.

Moist lips are beautiful prefix.
You can detect the taste of ripe pineapple

Warm curvature of lips
they take you out to the edge.

What makes you love me more than another?

There are photographic shots of you naked,
you were looking over your left shoulder, as if
someone had caught you inside a brothel raid.

You do not see the background, but between
the bed and the door, a window facing deep
percussion of ocean.
Is our bare image
transparent film of skin
painted or imprinted, she asks.
Both of us projected on the inner wall
coming home naked through wetlands.

PLACES SHE RETURNS
TO WITH EYES CLOSED

You are the man who finds me in a stranger's
house at noon, and juggles gunpowder
tea in painted tin cups

the stranger who lets me fall asleep on your
shoulder
on a commuter train bound for the
City.

My thigh accidentally touches your thigh,
on a ferry, on a bus, in a plane,

And I share a taxi to your hotel room.

Your eyes are the same color green as mine.
I am making a bed with a man I have never seen
before . . .
and it feels like we have already kissed.

*a voyeur watching my hands as they travel over
your bed, my voyage and you are watching me
make it.*

I smooth sheets of linen, you can read every word
written underneath.

Are they love notes?

I make a flute—whoever hears
a faint song when I play late at night.

Or have I traveled too far away?

I touched a bird that had swallowed red arsenic
I rubbed my hands over its breast—
now everything I touch becomes invisible.
Can you find me?

I burn grass to ash.
Mixed with salt, the water taste like sea foam
I save a cup for you.

Do you come with the room?

I do.

The man I run to when I am lost
leave the stage

The Man who carves a whale bone into a hook
ties it on a string around my
neck.

The man who loved me on a whore's mattress
in a student house. A room
full of freesias stolen from a garden
while dogs were barking
winter night waiting until dark,
our shadows together in streetlight sea fog.

Who brushes my long hair when it was tangled in
an opium room.

It is you, lover.

And slowly unties laces on leather boots,
you had undone the first knot,

when I
found you kissing my inner thigh.

The man draws with charcoal
traces my heart in sand with driftwood
the man who sleeps with me
holds me in his arms, I am tired from
everything I do not understand.
the sound of your voice makes it all right.

I look into your eyes.
I want to tell your beautiful face to hide from
growing older.

Lover, you are destiny and my world. Build a
fortress with towering buttresses.

Can we keep love in and shut the world out?

If you stay, he said.

And when I begin to know you, I am not sure if
you are my disciple, a pilgrim or a slave sent like
sleep to erase my own
thoughts.

Was my stone jar of dreams adulterated by you?

The sound of a faraway dog
wakes us in the barking.

Don't get me wrong, I love this dance we do, but
sometimes together feels like intractable marble
with love written there forever like a resonating
prayer.

Promise no erasure of us, no arguments found between us.

There is no war we belong to: the Lover said

I see leftovers of time on your face,
ashes, sand,
after things are broken
and scattered
something you swallowed in the sea,
fragile

shells handed to you by a woman
on a faraway beach
nautilus found a hundred fathoms deep.

You run them around your fingers.
In the ruins of us all
they remain for a long time,
like inky souls
reminders of forgotten things.

The woman you touched
still here
her scent held as salt on the shell.

There is a myth of monochrome.
Some things appear pale white, but have pink pigments.
Marble faces of saints were covered in pink paint.
Now the place is filled with ghosts
driftwood and baked clay
the color of sunset before it slips away.

****

If you borrow my shadow and walk away
farther than I had been
would you find your way back
without a compass
tell me what you had seen?

I will put these prayers in my shoes
and walk a thousand miles
with my eyes closed
farther than you can dream
but I'll always come back to you.

The Havana cat watches us in the waking.
Cinnamon paws in smoking grass
from sun-thaw.
Between pavement cracks he leaves a message
there are cat flowers...cat-tail, catmint, catnip,
cat's paw,
arrowed in concrete.
Look closely at furry corners of his mouth
you see the old cat smile.

PART III

THE ART OF LOVE

An Artist's trace is memory charcoal.

In the afternoon you teach me to draw primitive
secrets of breath and space
I will draw your wrist where heart beat pulses
to spine.

Where do you want me to lie?

Wet charcoal turns to black like earth rocks burn
in winter fireplace.

I feel heat when you stand close.

Dark prints of you begin as dreams
like coal ash on fresh snow. Some fingerprints
indelible, some delicate, some
fingerprints hard bruises you never wipe away.
Like watermarks when you hold paper up to
the light.

Inside paint. In ink.

Does what we see have more layers?

Life-model in your room,
ghosts behind ice glass inside my dream.
Stories not as history, the way things remind you
a place, a person, time,

photographed priests preserved in gold,
warm blood emptied shell on pavement,
rusty placenta planted under a native fern,
the small boy
turns around and leaves
a wedding dress left at the train station,

repeating monk-bone mantra for luck,
cherries for a fuck, lace lost under the bed,
catching piper fish in a net, frangipani lei around,
fucking as a commuter plane flew over us.

Then I interrupt you in thirty years...
The sea came in a tidal wave last night,
rosary of love
making sacred foam
how a woman knows him.

****

You should know, part of me is held
hostage by you,
whatever you know about me,
the robe I wear is your cloth now,
the secrets & surges in the cells of our bodies,
blind grinding of belly & hips are formed by
hands,
not our own.
I felt it happening.

Slowly draw thumbs out towards the center
and down inside thighs repeat strokes over and
over moving from the beginning, up, long
movements. Then smaller curves,
drawing invisible lines around sides of lips
between. I felt it happening.

With fingers spread, brush with flat of hand
out to where you began.
Small brushing strokes with your
thumb working upwards
thighs between river
bed. Lighter so your touch is

now the passage is
wet with scented rain.

... is warm delirium.

Dark roses you gave me wrapped in rough paper,
what is kept between us
in the moonlit galley turns to silk & charcoal
of naked drawings of you on the floor.

You add gold leaf to first painting; wet canvas
in a public gallery
makes love to her with his tongue
in the private room.

Who was she?

I etched a woman on magnesium paper.
She posed for me in the drawing room
There were jeweled eggs scattered on the table
a small dog sleeping
in her lap
She was there, like Rumi's child
her day dreams well hidden.

I traced roses on delta of her bare shoulder.
And I realized she had my eyes.
She had my eyes on her breasts, on her shoulder,
and in her
moist lips were pink vibrato
she made them as one
warm curvature out to the edge
her image painted on the sky.

The ghost of Havana cat watches her pull the slik
slip—then chases a butterfly.

It was a winter rain again that day.
I etched copper plate,
wanted to unbutton her military coat.
But I stayed away. Later, your Father threatened
to kill me.

(in aqua ink).

Scratch zinc plate; recover her naked image,
and then you reproduce her,
lines on paper, hair washed beyond sepia,
a bracelet around her ankles
every body is dilution, pores of paper skin
now a stain, not in her vein— but memory
paper sheets have sharp edges
you bleed into margins.

The wound in life is where two edges meet.

Kissing in the secret chamber
we become our own sustenance
I taste salt that has been sent with us
like pollen from infinite oceans.

Can I ask you this

if you no longer loved a woman, what would you draw?

I would draw a body of river and rocky
mountains. I would draw the odor of opium,
burning blue in poppy fields.

The canvas closest to you, I left empty.

All empty canvasses are thoughts

I hear whispers from
moon outside the window. And in the bedroom.
A tattoo indelible, lock of hair,
transparent face of a lover
the look between us
when our eyes first meet, I felt like
we had already kissed.
Unmask me; let me keep my eyes open to you

no one else who makes me feel this way
there are rocks in our bones, a river running
through our veins,
if we left each other now, my body would rattle
in emptiness.

Do you love me?

I have never loved a woman more than you.

Will you protect me from this?

I am afraid of spiders, living with lies, and
lightening. In the distance a man hears violent
thunder crashing as if the splitting of an
hourglass, cracking of time.
The warmth of his body against mine,
familiar now even in dreams.
His arm around my belly, the weight of him
holds me in.

Indigo morning. The end of the month where
September falls into October.

It was four thirty in the morning, when I saw him.
I was riding in a taxi cab on the way to the
airport.
A man walking barefoot, he carries two feather

pillows,
the sleepwalker escapes from one dream to
another.

Harmony in spheres, sun and moon and
planets move in rotation: the Ghost told him.
Still he asked the question of the moon: is there
a man leaning on a fork carrying a bundle of
money? Or is what
you see, a man holding a thorn bush? Or burying
ashes in the sand? Or fishing for a whale in a
bucket of water? Or a man coveting a casket of
gold? The answer is on the engravings of silver...
someone left the argent blank.
Someone left the mirror by the door.
A ghost writes in the mist and places it opposite
the sleepwalker. Then he reads the inscription
reflected in the sleep-walker's eyes.

How do I find you?

I was sleeping in the garden, I promised to wake
when I laid down
the journal, page open at the last word
I wrote a phrase about the river
the depth of an ending,
something about you
your paint blistered boat.
Some oak planks shaped like a relic.
One was almond.

The day I left the gate open.
I did not plan to stay so long.
Until the monk's voice whispers
 a prayer tied on my finger,
in the first days lest I forget
a string tied to a faraway kite

in the remaining days
ghost of goldfish swimming
in bowls.

The Havana cat returns for good. The sound of
claws scratching
glass like an apple
twig.

A ghost rubbing against my ankles
His fur is cold brown
fog.

Filling your bowl thin cream again.

There is a myth of monochrome. Some things
appear pale white, but have pink pigments.
Marble faces of saints were covered in pink paint.

Now the island is filled with ghosts made of
driftwood and baked clay the color of sunset
before it slips away.

UNIVERSAL QUESTIONS

You make up question, the way you make up
answers. But what you believe is what you
imagine.
What illusion
a tomato is a love apple, an incandescent moon
magnified through a weatherglass, so far away.

A photograph of a man in receding landscape,
he is wearing a tartan turban, as if he is the ghost
of an Indian Gherka, standing with his woman in
the tea garden,
fan palms and lime trees, they planted a hundred
years ago.
The odor of grass, mint and curry plant
crushed with bare feet as they walk
down by the boats
blue buds are swollen, bursting
open
down in the bay, the ghost boat is an open skiff.

He carries her across the marshes at low tide,
like a bride leaving a chapel, her arm over
his shoulder, head buried in his neck,
his skin smells of salt moss,
the way he carries her, the hem of her dress stays
dry,
flounder flapping under his feet cool like leather
sole,

he leaves no footprints.

Touching you with bare feet

as if my sole is walking on you.

gold smuggled in hem of my skirt

poems smuggled in the hem of my skirt

A photograph of the fable, taken long before I was born.

My Grandfather's secret journey.

I can see from a ghost image, some beautiful origin of you, the Lover said.

PART IV

THE ARTICLES OF EXPOSURE

I heard a Saint enter by the pavilion; leave us
crumbs so we will not starve.
There are empty baskets and blank roads ahead.
Bread crust. Orange peel.
If survival is an unbroken habit, would I steal
from you...
just to eat?

I will give you half my oranges, you said.

Warm tangerine in your pocket
walking on the night road
nothing under my skirt.

If your mouth is a vessel, your lips are
the rim. *Violet cherries she holds*
inside her mouth,
her tongue is the stoning, crush of scarlet, stains
your lips
mauve litmus of lovers.

I want to fall into your life, suck your stone, spit
pips and bite the core.
Juice you. Seduce you.
That is what I want to do.

You are my water bearer in the tropics, do you
notice, the closer we get to the Equator, the
thirstier we become?

I kiss you again

the taste of salt.

What was it you found between the crystals?

The correlation between us. A study of sex.

I know the feel of your body with my eyes closed,
I feel you
in my sleep. And I feel you sharing my shadow
in the hollow of my self.

In an old Venetian mirror the silver backing,
smoky
and torn.

Do you see yourself as you want to be seen?
Touch me as you want to be touched.

The mirror in our room holds history inside,
does it run out of reflections?

In your room, floor to ceiling drapes drawn back
over dusk,
your body still beautiful
as you close curtains over the windows
sunlight is a torch, dust dances through a slit
where two fabrics touch.

Fragrant ice melting on your tongue
crushed peaches & sugar cubes
the ghost of champagne
sweet foaming mouthful
of kiss.

I want our moments to stay—like this.

Submerged woman meshed inside a semi dream
touching thighs, temple wall under her knees

A rosary of clitoral bead.

Blindfold him.
Cloth wraps your eyes... let me trace you
Moving the circumference, follow the map.
Unmask him: let him keep his eyes open to you.

Fire burns blue unicorn light
lily paint is scented Venetian white
silk quilt left an imprint of us,
as if a light rain had been
falling.

The artist paints a rusty box then nails it to the
wall.
It was confessional amplification;
the box saw everything we did that night.

Observed, absorbed and stored memories inside.
The artist explains: Art absorbs us, memories and
desires
translate to paper or canvas.

An artist and woman exposed.
You and I hold energy, like rock & sea together.
In bed, I reach for you, the way a swimmer
returning,
reaches for shore.

Looking back through a camera lens.
An image of you
Reflected in cupola
Wet fingers vibrating her rim
butterfly alights on the rim
tinsel thin shows traces of sin.
The wing of brimstone butterfly
all cellophane and Baleine Sea
Double cups of pearl and silver,
emptied without a a drop being spilt.

Kiss is warm and perfumes your wine.

Later you tell me to destroy all negatives.
Did you? You know I don't do as I am told.
I keep photos of us inside an envelope
negatives of us naked, I said.

Late afternoon sleeping under a ceiling
carved with slivers of stars,
every shutter closed from the street
no one knows who is inside this room.
The art dealer told me you were a painter of
women and religious icons.
He has a special gift for rendering, she said.
The tear drop he paints, still wet.
Painting her body, the way she lay on linen sheets
brushing foreign light and black together.
She knew you well.

I am not jealous of women in charcoal, laying
naked on your heavy gauge

paper, the lines circling nipple, how you trace
between her legs with wax

crayon when you draw her in, just the way you tie
up her hair

when you smudge wet & saliva you use
in the rubbing
the black leaves me breathless.

I never slept with anyone since you—
you will always be my woman.

But I saw the same green eyes in another

photograph.

You photograph a woman carrying bundles of
sticks on
her back.
she carries fire & wood.
Alone road where verdigris grass hems shores of
Lake Limone
bruised lemon wood, her only perfume.

You try to save someone...you save this
photograph of her.
After a while, you forget what you are saving her
for.

Images of people are hard to destroy.

PART V

FRAGMENTARY THOUGHTS

Another weekend we carry the whore's mattress
down the mountain. We hold red kapok, pressed
thin by rivers, above our heads.

We are gardeners, ancient dirt embedded under
our nails. In prints of fingers, we leave a stain.
Everything remembered in the dissolving we find
each other waiting for the traffic lights to turn
green.

We walk through streets, hidden under the
mattress for two miles, stopping to lie down
on pavement when we begin we fall down instead
of upwards like angels climbing down from
mountains, office workers detour around our
mattress, we walk gold pavement to a cave in
Corinth, we are looking for love
in the chapters, from there you can watch the sky
turning deep burning sunset, when we lie in the
same bed no one can tell if we are dreaming, our
eyes shut facing each other, your breath warm in
my hair.

The things we carry when we move to the studio...

Blue bird in a cage, an old brown cat, cartons of
books,
sable brushes, charcoals, double patchwork quilt
from salvation army. French pastels in ballet
colors.
Opiate of perfume mingles with your aftershave.
Together in a leather suitcase, your shirts sleeves
strangling my intimates.

Some images are hidden, some images are
transparency, angora jersey, silks, cotton & mesh
you don't know my fabric yet

unlace, untie, unbutton
undo all of me.

We paint bedroom walls with sun, yellow rays
drying by late
afternoon, the way sepia light holds warm
shadows

we enter the desert room.

Touchstones
pressing your lips into mine,
some breathless collision
happens.

We stand in another garden,
late afternoon sun pouring down bedroom walls,

jars of yellow jonquils,
the sleep of spring bulbs,

a sound not only of leaves but the pouring

of water

down

from the rim of heaven,

our bare feet leaving footprints ... on the edge of
the earth.

Paper fish

a woman strings pearls with her lips
the voices of fish

the roots of a mountain
the spit of birds
tongue buried in sacred games
remembers her mouth

A stone holding its own weight
we were lovers holding each other
warm in the unfolding

there was a garden of silk
soft buds of fabric
perfumed like violets

balsamic of kiss
slips from lips

every seed is given away
to another part of ourselves
in the incense of heart
we become sleepers of each other.

Twenty one grams
the weight of a soul
unhinged
the growing wings move forward.

In the kitchen

On dusty wood shelves, preserving jars, sweet
beetroot, lemon & orange marmalade, scarlet
tomatoes in brine, baby onions, melon rinds in
sugar syrup.
A library of summer fruits & vegetables, pickled
& preserved lined up in alphabetical order,
archives dating back
before we were born.

Someone left them there.

Artichokes are first summer vegetable to ripen on
the roof garden. A yard out back, intimate pocket,
city backyard we rotary hoe, grow sweet corn
high as your shoulders, broad beans turn black
with sooty fungus, in deep corners
buds of marijuana.

In winter, you leave oven door open

to warm our kitchen, blue bowls with fish
swimming

porridge & dates,

pecans & grated brown sugar.

When you exhale, every breath comes out of your
mouth is iced smoke.

An illusion in a Magician's book
because my teeth are cold in the city: said the
blue ocean bear,
spooning another helping of porridge.

(Your winter hand cold like fish)

How long will you hold your breath
in a bowl of water for me?

I can teach you how to drown, he said.

Take one breath underwater
and swallow one more mouthful
then you sink into water

the sea inside you
on your lips

The radio woman singing
her voice was yesterday's ocean...
after a while, you find what is most deeply mine
make this our song, make it touching
make the words part of me, like the sea is
silver diving bell
sometimes you tarnish delicate things, just by
breathing.

(I asked you)

What would you have carried back then?

A photograph of you when you were younger
you were not weighted down—I carried you
across the grass
on my shoulders.
(how much lighter you were barefoot)

Some smiles I knew were counterfeit.
(blue album, embossed with starfish & ocean)

Where do old photographs go?

I hold onto images, as if the album is inside me
now,

a woman, hair drawn up with
flowers & tortoiseshell comb
cotton missionary dress & lady finger bananas,
plastic leis hanging in windows & fly-paper
streamers from the ceiling & Christmas lights
blinking & skinny dogs wander
the streets, none wearing collars.

Later you make a print of her on rough paper.

Someone left magnetic poems
on the refrigerator door

it is not about love but attachment
when we are younger

we attach one thing to another
orange marmalade, sourdough toast & tea

lie around in bed with me.

I could love this man secretly long before he
wakes.

His eyes do not see. Dark lashes
enter his
space, slow tracing down long bones, curving
into her
halcyon lover you ignite heat with your lips.
He kisses my throat. Slowly...you touch
secret places.

Tracing and retracing

He does not see women watching. Wanting to
steal sex with him.
If I look their way, they will break me with their
eyes.

I come moist at the touch of you.

When we pull away, nothing separates
then my hair unraveling over your thigh.

Am I dreaming this?

Boulders at the far end of the bay are warm
from a day of sun, holding our palms open, like
children applying invisible paint
with outstretched hands.
When you cut open rock, you unearth bones
that belonged to fish.
My fingers smell of fish. When you live on an
island,
everything smells of fish
The phosphorescent bone of a snapper A fish
within a fish
I wait for you on the beach
you taste of salt after the wave breaks.

Our tents erected some distance from the Ark. I
can smell rough tar, ironed sheets and camphor
wood from faraway
places; hear the roar of animals tied together. Or
is it stone
bucket sound of waters rising?
There are waves curling at the bottom of this
cartography page. And the faded colors are old
dyes, berries and vegetable colors,
I like the idea that a map of a place is edible.

If you were lost, to be a survivor, would you lick
the map with
your tongue—your last saliva?

I would share juice with you.
Like a mouth telling its
secrets, the Lover said.

They would find us, our tongues inked purple
last thing on our lips—was myrtle.

What would you miss if I was gone?

Your eyes, I would miss your eyes.

I know you—like I know myself
the way you are about to cry, sometimes
but then you blink.

In this heat you can't see through distances.
But lately, I feel as if someone is unraveling

what was the future?

endings & beginnings are all the same,
all arbitrary, all unreal,
all illusion

night is not what the night is,
it is what we make it: he whispers

One last thing...

I don't want to die alone

Promise me this...

*If you go before me, leave the door open with
your shoe.*

PAINTED CHRONICLES

1 / 1

How do I cross the Bridge of Gold?
The bottle answers with the sound of broken
glass.

2 / 2

There is a monastery buried in sand.
Belfry ringing notes as we pass in the desert.
We do not see
The ghosts of priests pulling the rope.

3 / 3

The gilt edge prayers book left in the gutter.

Is this evidence or artist's geology, the wound on
the Saint's tonsure?
All of this I painted.

4 / 4

Even the purity of outlines. Double portraits
posed before the river.

Does it pre-date man and stone bridges?

Once the river was damned with barrier rocks,

but in the portrait
her hair falls like water.

5 / 5

Facing each other. A man is mirrored by a
woman: he smiles.

6 / 6

A woman's base passion is her salt imagination:
he said
ringing a hand bell out the side

Window.

7 / 7

There are heathen stones scattered like gray sheep
and too
much tin in rock waste.

But in my orchard, fruit grows on branches,
perfumed, luscious with juice.

I want to be your harvester. Juice you.
Seduce you.

8 / 8

Through your life, Lover, do you feel rare
accumulation, you meet someone over; find them
again in a room of many.

Dip your fingers into sacred
what is yours, is mine
what is mine
is yours: she whispers.

There are many rooms with only one key,

like a fish hook
she swallows it.

You tell a story about the bride of the sea
the lover throwing the gold
band ring into the sea, shouting.

A bride swimming away from you. Her dress
floats like a Venetian island.

It was Ascension Day when I looked up.

UNIVERSAL QUESTIONS 2/2

What happened with your absolute first partner?
First sex was like the taste of mango.
I did not know what I was eating,
It could be sweet. It could be poison.
It could taste like nothing at all. It tasted so good,
I didn't care.

Without touching, bodies sense random heat
my naked flesh.
Some hallucination happens.
Secret images of bodies surrendering
carnal imaginings of a stranger's body we have
yet to know.

Later, my first love returned to the woman with
dark satin hair, the one who wore layers of lace,
under a skirt with French knots
she embroidered with red silk and a mattress
needle curved
like a bow.

a blonde man and his cross-eyed child.

I saw them at the crossing.

Summer house Black Rock. Wild grapes grow
there.
Trailing vines strangle peach trees in the old
orchard.

Our bare image
always takes the same route

transparent film of skin
painted or imprinted

My body balancing against box tree: how random
foliage imprints guilt on bare shoulders.

What impression will I leave on you?

A garden behind a hedge. Root vegetable planted
in rotting seaweed, random rows pink gourds and
summer squash. Warm sun bone magnifies on my
thigh.

Before we push through this immoral interlacing,
folding pliant
end of cord, our ankles tied together
we are not tame
caught intoxicating each other
sexual fuse outside the window.
Then long voices traveling down the pathway,
tripping us up.

A double knot on each
side and two ends, interlacing, interwoven.
The way you bind me

silver bracelet on your wrist
a box of wood covered in gold leaf
a small piece of paper, before

you tied wild grass around my wrist.
A double knot on each
side and two ends, interlacing, interwoven.

The way you bind me.

Come back to bed....
Your voice is warm stone.

I found a lifelong taste for you, your voice filtered
in my throat; I breathe you
out, my lungs fill again with the breath of you,
fossils of our time, sometimes

I feel a palace of glass fish bones, breaking inside
my heart.

I want to stay a while, back in your childhood
bedroom, looking through a small boy's dented
cigarette tin: spool of string, razor blade, postage
stamps, bluebird eggs, drop of your blood on
microscope slide. See through the cellophane of
a fly wing magnified. Burn a hole through paper
with the sun.

The cardboard gap where your fingers dislodged a
match, a photo of your black dog.
His head tilted to one side as if he is listening.

Tell me the secret?

I was the son of a fireman and a book keeper.
They named
me after a dead uncle
I would rather have been named after a dead fish.

I touch the scar on your knee

Tell me?

I was a small boy jumping over barbed fence.
Barefoot boys on faraway roads
chasing dogs across
wild borders.

He touches the line on her finger

A small girl holding a carving knife.

There was a child's swing in the garden
I used to spend summer days
swinging without touching the rope
I took turns with no one.

Were you lonely?

Sometimes.

Names of girls you once knew?

First kiss?

Girl on grass tasted barley sugar.

She was an orphan.

We grow up remembering . . .

Do red battle wagons and sky rockets still exist?
There are bi-planes blue and red flying in
cumulus.
Some days of primary colors, how blue is closest
to heaven,
and clouds look like sheep.

A boy. His lips blowing through tissue and plastic

comb. Remember tunes you played once as child,
when destiny was
a place ahead of you and no shadows hid behind.

And all you felt in that moment was your own
breath, through paper, vibrating your lips like a
kiss. And you were you,
in that moment, making music was all.

Ears are seashells with fish shaped cochlear
bones. Lined with silk they reverberate.
From a distance, you hear falling waves, head on
a pillow,
you hear the weight of ocean.

Enter the composition.
Against folds of white-washed wall, statue
shadows are deeper. Looking further back
a mother swimming past the breakers.

Read the sky with me like you did as child

How the arms of a mother wrap you in childhood.
Always a floating blue gown.

She wraps you in a thick towel until you
are a small cocoon;

She picks up the bundle of you, kisses
blonde curls of hair

her young one, light and small... how fragile your
folded wings.

Still, you leave her.

Remember moments before you traveled the
world alone? There was always someone to help
pat the lid of the bucket turn it upside down,
tapping until tin from sand you pulled off the
castle and the turrets were perfectly formed.

Rock pedestal steps down to Saint Leonard's
Beach, kauri planks, kudzu grass,
sand grains roll upwards over the dunes.

I followed a boy running, his feet stamping wet
sand, placing bare feet inside his footprints.

His feet stopped at the edge of the sea.

A blue jellyfish, swelled my bare feet and
someone
carried me home.

Looking back at the abandoned beach, I think
the boy was you.

As a small boy you dream the journey over
oceans to faraway islands.
What was it you were looking for?

I was searching for gold, spices in ships, polar
bear mints in tins, a friend.

Finding dry water holes, climbing barbed wire
fences.
Finding out that the dream is nothing like the
dream
when time tips forward
when you grow up
A rusty battle-wagon left in the grass
the swing empty without you.

MONOLITHIC

A woman, while her eggs are destinies
night planet ovulating around loose stars
she belongs to the Chalk Man
fertility tattooed on raw earth
he wraps tundra mat around.

All grass was burning when I looked back

The author of human graves was watching me.
I caught his eye like fire on the hill...

I want to give memory rising out of flame trees
when I split them: he said.
Leave dying embers behind. Forget all that haunts
us.
But the end of all fire is charcoal. Compressed
between my fingers.

Her lover twists grasses he reaps
Barley man, thick plaited
this coupling is my talisman.
(He binds the ring on my finger)
a marriage ring of grass...

Someone throws white rice in the air.
It rains over our bed.
As if birds bathed in perfume flutter above us.
Drops of scent rained from their wings
on naked skin.

He breathes a woman's scent, intoxication is her.

Slowly my thighs close about your neck.

Chamois butterfly floats on her thigh
A pattern in a veil
nude stain of original sin
red fragment baked in sacred cake.

I am pregnant with your baby.

And the world sees the shape of a woman.
seed in her, wet as she was, caught in wild, hot grass.
A counterfeit moon rising under skirt.

His ear against her belly, he listens to the pulse of his child, a drum away. Conceivable now, he loves his woman this way. She holds holy water and his child.

Some welding of human parts some soldering of souls happens.

I awake with sand on my pillow.
You sleep like you float Lover
your body facing towards me.

You give me more than I need
and honey trumpet flowers wrapped in paper

You stab my ears with diamonds
some delirium happens when you change your mind

I dreamed the baby floating down a river
filled with blue roses: the Lover said.

His sculling first water

the palm of my womb holds him

holds its fingers closed like a hand.
On nights where there is no moon, you count unborn stars in sky.

Women birthing are vast ocean and fire, consuming

her: all waves were burning.
a baby is born when winter wraps the country in cold on 21st July
umbilical root almost strangling your tiny throat, little boy
without maps you found us
your tiny fingers covered in wax like a long distance swimmer.

All women who give birth are Mothers.
All Mothers are named in the book.

Protect him in his cradle, take care of his words, bring him home safely, and look after him when he is out of my sight.

When you are born, life is arranged in alphabetical order, with porcelain bracelet tied to your wrist by the midwife.

A mother does not need to label her baby. She could find her child in an orphanage at night among all lost children.

You sleep between us.

A blonde boy lies naked
your features not yet hardened,
small body lying against
the man who shares the same name
holds him
in sun's warm enclosure, until the boy wakes
and disappears somewhere on the beach.

Biting the water fountain
your milk teeth
left under your pillow
throw school books
up in a tree
grow up and leave.

Summer...

You can smell summer in fields behind our home,
the sweet scent of apple blossom birthing from
trees outside our window.

I'll love you by the seasons

I hear whispers of lovers who slept before us.
We are not so new.

Ancient wattle walls, rough layers of wash are
painted lime then white.

Bleached essences hold sighs inside forged locks
close casement window shut. Almost airtight,
still summer has enough breath in the day to slip
between frames.

Inside, chalk walls rise like ancient cliffs from
flagstone floors. Black beams sag heavy over our
heads, hold ancient archives of lovers' words,

intimate filigree of wormhole wood.

Rusty nails hold Bengal roses to trellis outside
our window where sparrows lay tiny eggs and ivy
creeper binds between
thorns.

Handfuls of mallow pink fall on bare skin, on
linen sheets first initials silk scribed monogram.

I found another child in the dreaming
The night we pass into each other

A child floated down river, into my sleep I caught
her in my arms: he said.
She was wrapped in the beginnings of life.

I did not see her eyes until later

Then time tips forward.

A child reads calligraphy of clouds as snow
or rain about to fall.

to tell you before you left...

The highest clouds were gossamer that day.
Thin veils drifting thirty thousand feet
above her.

She read their prophecy,
of tiny ice crystals,
strong upper winds,
combing them out to feathers
words fly away like birds.

There were stalks of wheat in the sky, the day
she left,
the sun's rays forming a ring of light, a halo
around the solar disc
followed her as she went.

The beautiful cumulus girl
does not question the lack of dreams. Where there
is nothing to dream,
she dreams everything.

UNIVERSAL QUESTIONS 3 / 3

Gardenias—will she carry them in her wedding bouquet?

Will she place them on my grave?
And then she is gone.

When someone leaves, what are you left with?

Does your prayer come from the Latin word "to beg"?

Are there holes in memory?

There are images of you sneaking into the white out

we were invisible to the snow geese flying above us. Their feathers shredding atmosphere.

Wild birds keep others in sight by following the path of one in front. A
rhythmic formation,
some communion felt through bonds of heat.

A mountain dangles upside down in the sky I saw red cliffs mirrored along the wilderness of glass.
I believed in mirage,
instead of miracles, the milk-white fall of paper snow, shaken under a dome of glass.
Paper weight of rudimentary dreams.

You do not promise the bird in the sky, but give a wave of your hand
looking down a bird does not see the fabric of us.
Silk and lace on snow.

You look beautiful as my bride, he said.

In the photograph of the marriage cake, what do you see?

White sugar doves with blue wings landed in snow, clusters of eggs like silver moons dusted in palest blue.
There were marzipan crows.
Sex pods of pagoda tree, peacock flowers two hearts, Bird Cherry love & double snowdrop, white violet, red emotions & water lily sensuous. Amazon orchids, my epiphytic obsession & blueberry pollen blown through a straw for luck.
A veil of lace covers your face, each stitch an embroidered thought.

I promise to love you always.

A snow bird nesting in tall trees, he looked down as we were walking by the river. A bird sees twice. looking down on the speck, he sees two human beings. He shifts his weight, blinks black eyes; a sacred bird looks straight back at us. He sees us as one small speck, walking a straight line, hears the language of fish, feels the mountain rooted in earth,
from a distance, the parting of water, how the seams shift in opposite directions.

Held captive by water.

A human body can not last
Seven days without drinking.

We are all vessels.
The way we hold each other.
The way I contain myself.

Can we go back and find simple rooms of our
past? I said

I want to find you again.

In the house you find traces of us.

When you leave a room, part of you remains.
We go back to the streets, looking for rooms we
both slept in.
The room is a garden of ginger and opium.
There are tiger skins on the path & white lilies
Leave your shoes at the door, Lover.
Sleep with me on the ground.

I was looking for a lover. Was I looking for you?
I left my ticket in a city & I left the city behind.
A passport with empty pages,
going no places you remember

You remembered
a million hours ago
first touch.

He smiles: wild on your lips.
A risk don't you think...you should never take
from a stranger.

But I do not always do what I am told. You

should know. there is more to life than netting or
un-netting.
Rules are unsettling. That is why I avoid them.

I did not know you were staying, he told me later.

Dogs bark.

When we go back to the rooms we loved in,
someone demolished the walls.

The shadow of a whore stood watching the bricks.
She was smoking a cigarette, a box-shaped
waitress, hair of steel, her turquoise eyelids open
and shut like enameled buds. Apron heavy with
the weight of flowers, where cobwebs catch small
flies but hornets and wasps break free.

*She wanted to buy pleasure: crotch snap, leopard
skin, black leather, put together, see right through,
mesh, penny in the machine, black lace me, street
walking, fast talking, dream, be the queen, satin
poky machine, and creamed trash, ask me again,
erotic encomium, come again, silk wrapping you
up like a birthday treat.*

She watches young men build a highrise. where
the backyard had been, walls red pitted bricks,
each brick shaped by convicts before the bridge
connected the shore, the edges of the walls worn,
where masonry wasps leave tiny dried marbles of
spit & red powder.

She has forgotten the faces of the men who came
to see her
on a mattress, there was no other bed.

All men want to touch her, They take her body
inking carnal prints, touch secret places inside
her, travel her silk road.

Someone is scraping ash from your eyes.
Some grains caught between your fingers, warm
breath, he blows them away.

The way you were covered up,
when red ash rained from the sky,
your hand reached up,
your palm touching the ribs of a sleeping dog.

All I wanted was to be admitted through doors of
the Church that holds religious
mannequins, blue robe, red oils dried below
thorns.
I repeated prayers worn out by sinners, a strangle
of rosary rope. But I was baptized in another font
brackish water sourced from an underground
well.
The last time I saw her was carnival day. She was
throwing horseshoes at a row of carved wooden
saints.
Out of the tent into the Jehovah comic, distract
the lion catch yourself by the tale, distract the
beast, with a broken chair, shaking hands with the
liars again, holding gold in a hand, oak tree on a
rock belongs to the dead, tree on a rock belongs
to the fable, running down old roads forever,
while we fall down, get up, fable and loss in
chaos, you were born by accident in a night of
shot down stars, a moon washed by night oceans,
we are orphaned in a city of memory. In the house
you will find traces of us, an incense burner with
warm ash, the stain of human seed seeps into the
woven mat

the night the dogs start barking.

Shadows of sleepers cast on stone wall. Rough
dreamers under olive tree. Shadows of sleeping
dogs cast on stone wall. Who would have
thought? So many dogs sleep under olive tree.

What holds the roof above us, rain on the
papered ceiling, palm trees weak at the roots...a
boat
sinking in the lagoon
so much is storm
by morning a foreigner wrote a prayer
tied it on your finger,

the future was never completely clear

but your eyes always were: the Lover said.
Fresh green. Not the fake green on paint charts,
but deep green, where fathoms below, a diver
keeps going down forgets to surface.

I looked in your eyes, while we were skin diving,
we lost atmospheres, until we ran out of breath.

A photo of the diver and me sitting where the
pool was.
I keep this picture of you. It floats inside me
every miracle given away like an envelope with
secrets, I will save the secrets for you
and when nothing is left, by sucking water from
a stone, blood in my mouth the sound of rushing
water over
stone is sleep
until we no longer exist.

THE MUSEUM OF SMALL FINDINGS

You end up leaving clues and fragments I find.
Indelible, collections of crumbs and blue butterfly
wings, postage stamps, fencing wire, a shoe
washed up, watermark on bathtub, tumbleweeds
of dust, a morphed tattoo, old bruise,
photographic negatives, copper plate,
lip prints, footprints, imprints,

*A phosphorous bone inside a snapper skull. The
fish inside a fish. There is a thumbprint from a
Saint on the skin.*

Stains on my dress,
Stains. Of sweat, cherry blood.

Found objects mark separation.
A year belonging and unbelonging
The way things remind me
pressed flowers in your pocket.

The door is open.

On trestle tables there are shards of pottery where
I broke
each fragment
numbered with faded red ink,
clay coins imprinted
with a sign of the church,
rough tender to buy a way to heaven.
cracked bowl from a shipwreck, tracing time,

a gold earring shaped like a cinnamon cat. In the
museum of small findings there are glass cabinets
with butterflies, wings pinned to velvet.
Your last painting palette, yellow umber
cracking, and in a small drawer, remains of a
pink wax crayon you drew beautiful lips with.

A ghost passes through the museum window
our history caught between black print
your hands hiding your eyes
until a voice tells you:
what belongs to you is lost
what didn't ...is hidden.

In the market...
a woman smiles like she knew us

before.

Woman in sensuous folds of raw silk sarong,
tangerine, lime green with gold flecks of sunlight
was, tightly woven around her pregnant waist.

She is binding cilantro with water hyacinth twine,
tying bundles of sacred basil, sweet acrid, like sap
from interior rain, the polished white roots, roots,
wraps them in dollar bundles with raffia.

Bread fruit with green finger leaves, purple figs,
violet sugar plums, rambutan shells are spidery
red. Abui fruit is canary yellow, red caked rust on
new potato.

Fermata is heatstroke, these colors driving me out
of sleep years of white has put me under.

The man inside the tin caravan selling jasmine tea

in forty degree air waves that move in vibrations
of unequal heat.
Slow silver colloidal raindrops falling on the roof.

A girl, floral sundress colored violet, cotton wet
with juice of fruit, bare feet tough soles on hot
pavement,
throwing walnuts in the gutter,
watching them roll
down concrete drain.

In the market of small findings there are paper
bags filled with lemon myrtle & dried bush
tomatoes, a yawn of a white shark jaw bleached
by the sun.

The red belly snake crawls into the linen basket
she spits from her fangs, rusty nails pierce
bare feet, a dog bites, shadows on an x-ray, a
fracturing of bones, a split second through a stop
sign...we take familiarity for permanence.

I want to leave the market.
I want to go back into old bedrooms and fill them
with freesia and bright burning candles.
I want to love you new like strangers do.

Hold on to the weaving, the flax basket with a paua shell
lock, hold on to the stone carving of a wave, gold
leaf carved, plaited string that ties the bone hook
from the rib of a Moa bird, the moss and feather
shoes of a man who was pointing the bone in the
sacred bush.

Everything is left behind
the objects of our existence are unearthed by

others
soft sable brushes on my face
when all the clay is gone I open my eyes
when one of us is lost
we find a room inside the other

Leave word and I will follow

leave a clue for me so I know you are close by.

The exact moment we change? I ask.

When we are lost for breath

when our dreams burst like clouds.

Male sapphires are closest to indigo
females are blue of heaven
jewels in turban sky.

Last night, dreams of a wild dove
passing over, black wing-bars opened like a fan.

He was passing through time to eternity

Did he give you a message?

A band around his foot is a ring of innocent, gold
purified in fire.

I read the inscription: We are hunting for clues
but none are given
we are reading each others lips, but nothing is
proven, dead languages, laundry lists,
holy prayers, tea leaves

I don't know why
a man marks a name in the bark of a rain tree

I know what we shared, by the scent of you in my lap.

Original drawings in the sketch, the paper is rubbed smooth
someone else has been rendered.

There was a message tied to driftwood with dried gut.
When lost or partially erased, we draw close

on a mattress where your dreams used to be,
repeating monk bone mantra for luck,

Then I interrupt you in thirty years ...

I have never met a woman who reads one thousand ninety eight pages of mythology dictionary and makes love like a porn star:

I am reading words like stones

Unpolished tiger's eye, cinnabar red,
bloodstone, moonstone, amethyst and citrine.
Some stellar diamonds. Uncut with ordinary rock attached.
Jade... is closest the dragon
every stone holds power...it just depends what you choose.

What gift can I give you?

A bowl for offerings?

I do not believe in stones.

You look at the stone in my palm.

You do not take it away.

He threw marbles in the air and ran his fingers
over the empty bowl felt roughness under the
smooth glaze, a trick of touch. the porcelain dish
is cracked underneath.

Yet he fills it with water.

A woman's passion is her salt imagination.
A Priest said, ringing a hand bell out of the side

window.

There are heathen stones scattered like gray sheep
too much tin in rock waste.
And always water in the water bowl.

No matter the damage.

THE FUGITIVE TEARS

Now I lodge in the cabbage
patches of the important
Not much sleep under Strange roofs
With my life far away...
— Osip Mandelshtam

They have stolen places I owned
our palaces
the lakes of my eyes
the river between us

the art of stealing so many
things belonging to me, stolen.

There is a cannon in the garden
surrounded by purple lilac
there is cold blood sprouting in his heart

I did not wish these things.

Our palaces towed on a barge
to the edge of pacific ocean
burned on the water all night
ivory gates open for cremation.

The outside places seem foreign
along my road
in an altered landscape
such places make me weep.

Is anything left

in a handwritten note about sadness
litter on a strangers lawn?
When the world wears a woman's tears
there are memories speaking
the abacus of wooden beads
each one smells faint sandalwood.

It's a trick of the visionary
an apocalyptic perfume of fate
like the candle end of time
I did not memorize these things.

They turned from an angel with wings of flame
to a soft grainy film
tarnished by tears.

After our children leave, this bed is too big for us
we are tipped out by ordinary things, banana and burned
toast,
a pinch of salt, how strong tea stains a white cup
by black tea leaves
and when I escape the fear of drowning,
I fear dying of loss
until I hear the voice I most wanted to hear
saying:

come back to bed.

You have an Angel sitting on the knuckle: the
Palm reader said.
My palm blue with ink; a lover's fork, a peacock.

But my Angel's have flown: I tell her.

Once they poured crystal buckets of water over
my skull.

Now I feel no tingle

A shot glass of happy was too much to ask.
They thought me too greedy.

Someone threw butterflies, a handful of iridescent
opals, blue jewels in turquoise shimmer.

The flapping of a single butterfly's wing changes
the weather.
Through
chrysalis skin, thin window panes, shapes of life,
emerald cocoon with tinsel wings,
emerge.

Catch a butterfly on the wing, hold in palm of
hand,
whisper a wish set yourself free.
The psychic told me all women are warriors &
angels with arrows and wheels of fortune turning
inside circle, the fortune will be yours, bags of
money, harvested like ripe wheat if you hold the
crystal tightly in your palm.

But she was wrong.

DECEMBER

Life, you deliver
Red letter rupture
One week before the Holy birth
No money for the angel now
An old Russian doll
Wrapped in gold paper
Her sad wings
Some feathery prophecy
A foreigner on a fir tree.

Fragments of text
From fractured tongue
Alien letters drawn
In calligraphic landscape Dark fears
Some are elongated
Shadows of blackened script.

Film his footsteps

The thieves on the road
In white cars
Are snow drifts
In disguise?

Covert eyes
Break into this house
Steal intimacy like rubies.

There are stones in our bones
A bloody river runs through
An electric fence of nerves.

FEBRUARY

It was the worst day of rain
The fire season was months away
A red dog barking

To a pencil river tracing
A map turned upside down
Last town becomes the city
And lost city is the town

Vertigo changes horizons
Like Lazereth waking in the garden
You only see what you have found
Love letters on microfilm
Wound
Inside the prayer.

Someone is always grabbing
Pulling off your shirt
Find it hard to believe
Man can rationalize this hurt

I can't go and tell him
I want another chance
I got to pretend I don't care
If he throws us on the street
And the people stop and stare

There is something about the future
 Nothing written down
But I keep it inside my head
I am left with secrets that we share.

I can't tell where we're going
Read the map upside down
The city is the country
And the country is the town

The cockroach in the corner
Hides in the keys at night
You only see him
When you turn out the light

Dancing in the ballroom
Orange juice stain on my dress
You wear the color of a collision
Someone photographed your smile
Took a long time to develop
You won't get it back for quite a while

There are roosters in the morning
They wake up much too soon
Make a black one friendly
woman breaks its neck

There is no need for crying
What's done is said and done
I can't work out the future
I start thinking
And then I want to run
To places in the desert
Places in the sun
I am staring down a deep hole
I stared down there before I was born

The man holds a thread
Attaches a bird to a ring But he waits
On a signal
All the birds dive in

There is no help for the hopeless
I used up all my prayer
Now there is no one left
To listen to the sacred
The verse about now and forever
the prayers they go too far

But the man is the river mouth
He is the ocean too
We are living by the water
Drowning by it too.

I said my shoes were holy
I can't walk on water
I haven't even tried
Now I'm older
Not so pretty
Can I hitch a ride

Throwing pumpkins on the road
The bamboo pole
You stick a hive and honey flows.

I'm holding onto hopeless
Thinking its my friend
Some friendship
I can't let you know
I rented this space
Long ago

I was looking at my fortune
Until the psychic came along
She promised me a home
And I waited
But she was wrong
She saw the faces
Colored up in lies

Twisted fact abrasions
Covered up his eyes

Now they've emptied all our money
Thrown us both away
How do you salvage something
When there's no one left to save
The dreams are all but faded
You no longer see the truth
Just a faint impression
Where the sky was
And the buildings touched the roof.

Your smile is all in pixels
Mine is in a frown
I was hoping for red paint and a wig
To make my mask a clown

I am laughing
I am laughing
I am laughing
Do you hear someone laughing
In a world upside down
The ceiling is the ballroom
I am dancing with a clown
Paper trousers
And yellow hair.

Shopping trolleys in the park
Wine bottles and plastic shoes
Greasy wrapping of fish and fries
No one remembers
So no one cries
The people on the park bench
Forgot the reason why
Push belongings in a supermarket trolley
Why they live outside.

MARCH

Can love hold us together through loss?

Change has a silencer
There was no scream.

We prayed for dew and danced for the rain
breathed in air of the sea
we were fish caught inside dreams
ghost palms broken by passing hurricane
now we are fugitives in this foreign land.

Basho told her:

If days become your living
 you are no longer poor

the reason for writing
the season for art

Walk for a hundred miles
straw sandals on your feet
the ragged men and clothes
of inmates in the city
of rubbish floating by a river
where exquisite dreams were sold.

Live in my shoes a while
then rags become a fur coat
when you keep each other warm.

Banana palm outside, water dripping

wakes the reed frogs
green as leaves in the giving.

a wood hut
a river boat
a tin shed
a brownstone house

Living in a room of lovers
hang a colored shawl as curtain
from the second floor
only bats & birds see in.

Pale faces of the morning
so many lips touching
good-bye
two buildings crumpled
skyscrapers to dust
close-up moments
of falling air
in a burning sky.

His rags of business shirt
both palms soldered together
if a prayer & pilgrims voice
finds its way back from hell
can we find a way back
as well?

If mothers could hear
through the ice window
hear us cry
sad days in the quarter
and ones yet to come
holding our heads above water.

Hold

an ocean in a jar
a photograph of you in my hand
we lay down in the path
of a summer hurricane
the way unnatural disaster comes.

In sadness we are jungle
iron bar and rock
the falling of an angel
ticking of a clock
time spent in the water
days left in the sun
desert water broken petals
and the rain was gone

Straw sandals strapped to our feet
when you walk the miles
you begin again
Look for answers in translation:
whispers a Persian poet
In a breath you find love...
but it hurts, Rumi
even your words open up
the wound.

Touch my sin
fever at the boarder
when I cross over
to your side
wrap sad bones in words.

The extreme cost of love
a night without a touch
when you forget the password
the enemy hands you a stone.

In parts, some images fall,

like mountain water
from a place, makes us afraid
deep inside the marrow
what is scattered
we could not see or name
the uncovered human face
hangs his head in shame.

TWO HUMAN ERRORS

1 . TO TAKE EVERYTHING LITERALLY

2 . TO TAKE EVERYTHING...

No...It is not hard to convince myself that the
place where men perish....could be true.
a place in the bleaching of bones where those
who perish
are collected as souvenirs by every passerby and
left in a heap. Bones are markers to show the way,
guide a road through
the desert for future travelers on the pathway
(no) birds are visible in the air, (no) worm or
beetle on the earth; traces of nothing.
And in places signs of life departure, piles of sad
bleached bones unidentified
as man or animal.

A LINE DRAWN THROUGH MID-POINT ON A CIRCLE

Some change occurs through motion

I have followed you not knowing where we would end—
until you reached a place I didn't want to go to,
where men perish when I looked in the direction of the horizon,
a sea of sand, extending as far as the eye could reach,

on the one side the sand formed high hills, like waves—my body

lashed into that position by storm; on the other side like the waters of
a still lake, rippled by the wind.
It was early morning when I dreamed I was leaving. I saw a
blue painted boat shaped like a relic. It floated on a smooth
sea. The cargo was silk fabrics
flying like tangerine kites in
the wind. I could not see your face
because the red sun was behind you. You seemed to be standing in fire.

The body is changed by the motion from moment to moment.

I was frightened. That is why I left you. I thought
I would rather risk death from destruction by
some fever-wind,
or starvation, rather than stay behind with you. A
fire
keeps you warm instead of a woman.

What enemy spoke to you with a mouth of death?

I will go first before many who still have to leave;
I will go in the middle of many who are leaving...
Look back to how
it was before I left you, look forward to how
we will be together.

Who authorizes such destruction back to nothing?

 I cross boarders holding a foreign passport.
Feet facing the door
as if I were already dead, carry me past the man
in the room. The gates
unmanned. I enter the house like
an unannounced guest. On the table, anchovies
soaked in lemon thyme and oil. Mountain
cheeses, sweet purple grapes.
In this room, you can detect the smell of ghost.
I open
a window so he can escape like a wasp.

My memory of the past and expectation for the
future, none of which can exist without you.

What stones do we need to rebuild our house and
how many.
What remembered pattern do we place them in.
Rows, herringbone, like an ancient road?

Find stones of many colors and after, I will name
the road after you.

By the passions of my body. Of carnal desires.
According to its own passions, as desiring,

It was early morning when I saw a man walking
barefoot on
the road. In the moonlight he looked like a saint.
He was carrying one feather pillow over his
shoulder. When the seams
split the feathers fell upwards reassembling into
lost birds & murdered poultry.

How long will it take until you can sleep through
the night again? To dream you are free from
anger's metallic teeth.

Does sacrificing this lead us to another place, this
fire-sacrifice, circus hoop

dragged us through beginnings.

I left you by cutting away.

This subtraction leads to nothing. For every
memory remains,
feels like heat in your body.

A body suffers by change, when love is taken
away from it, towards nothing,

although it can never reach nothing.

You move my thoughts by illumination

by telling the truth as you know it,
diffusion of light
this burning . . .

a flaming arrow fired towards a fixed point is nothing but an
impulse from the archer... the point reaches its end as though of
its own making. Our house continues to stand after the builder has built and water remains hot for some time after the fire has ended.

I continue to love you
after our house is gone.

I am fascinated by the way man plows in a straight line.
Straight lines, the memory of lines and the necessity for
man to have structure. If he does not plant his seeds in a line, then he
will not find them, they will be lost to him
how a plough moves, how man moves
his body
to seduce a woman in the field.

CONVERSATIONS
BEFORE LEAVING

You do not escape, someone lets you go, he whispers.

1 / 1

A wedding ring fits on my finger, sometimes the salve of divinity. Sometimes a slave.

2 / 2

I cannot stay living with you in a tent. It is snake season. The red belly black crushed on the gravel road will appear to be asleep.

3 / 3

Watching him through the soft jail of her dark eyelashes.
A woman sleeps until a man wakes her.

4 / 4

When you touch a Lover for the first time, something enters and stays locked inside then breaks when you leave.

5 / 5

Travel the distance like a pilgrim, until we reach iron crosses by the roadside.

The small dog, rescued by the woman who searched for ancient tombs, follows us. His fur holds Sahara sand, in his memory he sees the color of lonely, inside a cardboard box. A skinny puppy left to die
in the heat,
when she found him.

We find unexpected things when we loose our expectations.

There is a field of sunflowers. The heat turned them black charcoal in summer apocalypse.
Even beautiful things turn black.
Turn back, the Lover said

This invisible attachment we have for each other, hurts.

How did we get to this? There are photographs of us...
looking back to the beginning of us.

I sleep, like other woman do who sleep alone. At night I imagine I am held in the arms of sleeping men.

Sometimes the roof is filled with sounds of small animals that slip under clay roof tiles above my bed.
Did you get my postcards. Of wild flowers?
Of a naked woman, her body covered
in dried mud?

In my dreams I returned to our house, the

furniture gone, rooms empty. I passed through
walls like the vapor of ghost, only I am not dead.
I feel loss inside the walls, the overgrown
courtyard with moss between cracks of tiles,
the empty bedroom still held whispers of our
nights.

Last night I was dreaming I heard your voice in
my sleep. What part of you do you want me to
love first: you asked?
For a moment I felt your warm body, the weight
of you in bed.

How we transcend places to end up in bed with
the other in dreams—though thousands of miles
apart, I feel you sleeping next to me as strongly as
if I turned the light on and you are
lying there.

The soft indent of your head on the feather pillow
next to mine made me think we were going to
stay together always. Your body felt so close, I
did not look far into the distance, and you were so
familiar. You held my shadow
between your fingers.
In the bureau, shirts folded, socks rolled next to
mine, cotton touching red silk. We reached the
bedroom door, naked.

I want to tell you this.

When a man is away from softness, the scent of
his woman's perfume, the way her fingers run a
track up his spine...if you forget these things, if
you turn into sand, if the land parches you on the
outside...there is still a well inside where tears are
formed before you forget how to say my name, if

I return, will you know me. Will I know myself?

You can feel winter in the air, the way breath turns to personal fog when you exhale. Winter is returning to the countryside, bringing with her a history of thunder storms of such severity they throw the village in blackness. Candles & matches & a torch with batteries.
I don't want to be alone in the dark.

Closer and hunters' guns shooting wild hare by the river...
how did I get this far away from you, Lover? It feels like death reversed... the pain of sadness born because I am no longer with you.

It was daybreak when a half-naked man entered my dream and told me he was hungry. I offered him bread. He dared me to look into the distance. He told me he loved me
all I could think about was you.

I want you to follow me here. Travel the distance like a pilgrim, until we reach the place where locals place chrysanthemums on iron crosses by the road side. An ancient song about pilgrims, valor and bad
weather tramping through the Valley of Death. A grocery list in a ditch along the road written with a blunt pencil, something about a misspelled name scrawled on a half sheet of paper.
Everything fell from your pocket.

Lately I have been unraveling... what is the truth? A fly settles on my wrist. He senses the remains of blood. I left you by cutting away. And this subtraction leads to nothing.

For every memory which remains, feels like heat,
a body. God formed man from earth Genii.7.
The raising of
the dead and giving sight to the blind.
There are faces in the ancient stones. A man
caressing a woman in his arms.
When you look closer, you see.

Memory connects you back to a place, a room,
the perfume of lime twigs, and the scent of rain
falling on hot pavement,
to a person...another human being.

I scramble out of the same dream, French words
for river, where I met a stranger
in a bilingual dream. The room was empty,
except for his bed. Is anything left in a foreign
film about sex? When a man knows a woman,
there are memories speaking.

Much of life is about calculations you said. The
whole is greater than the part of us that is missing.
Is less when diminished and suffers when
something is taken away from infinite division
and towards nothing, eventually we reach
nothing without each other.

Saturn the highest planet, astronomers say is
fixed and permanent. God keeps certain things in
being, the way you kept me from leaving. Life is
a question of balance, you said.

I hold your door open with my shoe.

...how young

were you then and how beautiful: he said.

I keep the photograph of you next to my bed.
Your image is the last image I see before falling
asleep.

*I was seventeen in the photograph, lying across
your double bed.*

Some things break us, shatter our world to pieces
lover, I wonder will they eventually destroy years
of loving you.

You said you liked a woman with a sense of
adventure. I am a fixture in a foreign land. You
would not recognize me. When I look between
the crack in the tin mirror, I see
a stranger looking back.

What made us fit together?

Much of life is about calculations.
Measurements compared with measurement.
I count on my fingers.

*I do not to take more in my hand than I need to
survive. You can eat late summer figs from the
trees if you watch out for wasps, bread from the
market and eggs when the chickens leave.*

I said goodbye at the airport knowing I would
take this life essence conjured up between us....
does it remain like rare perfume in the room of
soul.

When you leave a place, any place, in the elixir
of last moments, the taste of apple & sugar
sweetened our last kiss.

Will this distance, this restructuring of our
material lives rot the heart of us?
Outside, purple figs are bleeding on the ground.
Wasps puncturing globes of fruit, the ground
beneath the tree purple, smells like earth's
summer jam.

The calico cat sits by lavender bushes, waiting all
morning to kill a small sparrow.
You do not escape. Someone lets you go.

Am I practicing separation to feel the levels we
exist on? Exist beyond the airline departure gate.
Altitude & boundaries of countries.

In the month where it begins.
Leather book, carbon pencil. Is this the scribbling
of a geographer...or traveler, or a woman who has
lost her compass?

FOSSILS OF US

1 / 1

The construction in a palace at 4am,
the sculpture of a woman holding the body of a
lover in her arms, chilled marble muscles on his
forearms, he was looking into her eyes.
There were no tears. The flood season was a
month away.

2 / 2

Her lips were faded, she painted them once.
And her lover kissed the red paint off.
Lips are salt plains,
a river running between the banks of a smile.

3 / 3

We are bound at the waist & thighs.
Slow drift of us is all we hold together
and shelter,
two lovers in the hotel room.

4 / 4

Your hair autumnal falling over fossil pillow
a forest of falling leaves, sleeping in his bed,
wild honey strands pouring between his fingers
warm earth fragrance of clay and moss.
You are not wearing perfume
when he buries his face
warm from summer

We find ourselves together.

Was this arranged by another part of ourselves?

What are we left with?

5 / 5

There are two children between us, a marriage, a
painting sold for an easel, her moleskin notebook
filled with numbered prayers.

6 / 6

Change your name before you leave here, the
Priest said.
We collapse under the weight of love: I tell him.
There is no one to challenge the truth.
Holding prayer stones for centuries, we fall under
the weight of illuminated text.

7 / 7

Can you write us Holy?

I will render your body's gold leaves and
luminous blue.
Leather cloaks drawn across you shoulders.
I will give one
a hunting bird who hears a single vocal cord.
He responds only to a one voice.

We will abandon words
as canvas is white, as tracings in wheat stamped
on earth.
Find circles back to beginnings. Paper seeds left
in the attic, a connection; splinters of us remain

...please leave someone to sweep up after we are gone.

What are we left with?

Memory keeps him hostage

8 / 8

In the market, there are cages of wild birds, their shadows perched on citrus branches.
And the journey of ghosts, walking through the market,
one lifts the door of the cage, birds fly up, landing on the hands of the clock. We take oranges from a pile until the weight of all rind falls, bruising the stones.

And a ghost hands you an orange and smiles.

9 / 9

Some mornings I feel like leaving you alone ...
Thinking of love and unlove. How we unravel love. Do and undo.
Tie & untie. Lock & unlock.
Last night I dreamed I unlocked the door and let my birds fly. But one dove was you and I never knew. Heart at his throat, vellum note bound with hemp thread. I read.
Lover: I tried to unlove you yesterday. But you stayed waiting
for my return.
Will you stay with me Lover?

for a while...

It was not my hotel
we were both visitors.
It has always been there waiting
wild flowers growing on wallpaper
as a room to be entered

I have looked the other way
closed the door
swallowed the stone

but then the door is open again.

I am lying on the bed
I have been here waiting for you
between the sheets
to find me
in the folding

We were never to be weighted down
warm stones entering our bodies
We build with our breath
and move in
tight secrets

I know the faraway corners
of you
my tongue is password
I enter your room
It is warm in there.
The moment we change the way we were
looking back at the house
in paper gardens each landscape
complete
we fill it
we move inside
broken bath house

canvas tent
rooms remember us when we were lovers.

You find sanctuary in places unvisited for years,
cool of church stones,
rusty prayers,
heavenly blue between leadlight seams,
always a shepherd girl clutching a lamb.
The blood red transparency of Saint's robe.
And Angels looking down, etched wings outstretched
they landed in clouds above us,
they were looking down
at you. sitting in the church,
the rain outside the door,
traffic on the road—
hidden inside stone walls.

City complacency sets concrete
in your spirit
and holds you under,
a long breath
Now certain currents move between
a highway you travel on.

I forget the connection to patterns & routines & layout of city

a monologue maker
makes me think...do I talk too much?

What were you thinking about just then?

A field of blue
The photograph I took of you
in a concrete city, wild flowers grew

shadows of blue
petals almost blue.

petals of cornflowers, iris, wood violets.

The woman collects blue cornflowers
Her blue saturates your fabric
like a cool shower

I see the obsession clearly

blue luck of birthstones
your attempt to separate sack
from diamond rock
and rocks
from sapphire
stones & dusted cinnamon earth: he said.

Jungle sapphire set in a wedding band
bluebottle glass
intrinsically valued on lined paper
inventory
and how someone
stole the Sappho stone
thinking it was sapphire he could sell
until she spoke
in a dream to Eros.

We are prisoners of each other,
an invisible rope attaches.
You think you can walk away
but then you take one step too far.

Night is heavy metal and shot down stars.

*Sometimes I worry about Malaria nights he
spends alone. Signs of art, of human existence,*

*black cave painting and thunder clouds rattling
with stones.*

Nothing has changed, but everything changes us.

I trace every footstep
a pathway back to bed
when we forgot how simple
go back to the start

I feel like someone watches over us

I have seen a woman who is
standing in the light
one of the most beautiful days
when you do not expect
what you have found
a different country perhaps

Looking out to sea with you lover
there is a new photograph of us
of flesh and silver nitrate
after the retelling
the voice of birds
unfolded in the flame tree.

He unbuttoned the garden of her cotton dress

I saved you butter pastries filled with almonds

Walking back to his room
like Jesus and the desert fathers...

She was barefoot on the stones

a photograph of her

developed slowly
soft blue light
in the photograph
she was facing away
an image of her
standing on the landing of the mountain.

It was a man who brought you down to earth: he told her later.

If love is the raw material, see me in a dream. The genesis of two traced back to the love affair.

If loving is a work of composition, you are the painter
If love is running its own course, swim the river.
I was born an island,
sharing the porcelain bath the waves break over us, slow burning salt bone in the bathhouse drifting out into shipping lanes.

Something survives of us a hundred fathoms deep on the way up to the surface holding kisses in our mouths like a skin diver holds breath, we were deep inside dreams
as counterweights of each other...one sinking
one levitating
striking into the water with our last match

lucky

We could keep each other warm at night, when the temperature drops twenty degrees below: the Lover said.

In dreams, men have disappeared, like snow melting, carving niches and pooling into void.

There are black and white movies of a woman:
walking away, fur around her face, her dark
eyelashes frozen white.

She films home movies, catching killer whales
with a lens. Dorsal slivers of mammals hunting
black and white Emperor Penguins.

Hold camera steady in sub zero, last outpost, end
of world. Core temperature, warm. External air
freezes. As she wipes breath fog away, gut sutures
on sealskin mittens scratch tempered glass.

You can read her words as ice, her mouth covered
with blue wool scarf. How celluloid shivers when
she projects arctic ghosts on his wall.

When he woke his hands were warm under her
body.

There are boxes from far away places and musty
sea chests from cold expeditions
where chill evolves unknown white & words
reveal nothing & silence is not recorded.
How two lovers stay warm, in the snow, the
falling snow.

There were memories of a harsh wintering over,
of uncomplicated survival. In silence as quiet as
speech bubbles,
I said, we need each other more.

*Fate means: to be facing each other and nothing
but each other and to be doing it forever: the
arctic ghost said.*

When the ghost speaks to you, does he speak in

words?

*A ghost said nothing, but I understood
beyond the wintering, how I see you in the white
out, is how I see myself framed as a ghost.*

*My soul wonders how I came to this, she said
looking out on water as if she was looking for
Jesus. Some inescapable loss feels trans human.
How do you cross
from here?*

You enter the river and swim. The fish inside the
fish, the sea inside the fish. We are salty, you and
me, once we swallowed an ocean, now the sea is
inside us,
we are floating and sinking at the same time.

He pulls a fish hook from my mouth and kisses
me.

Am I dreaming this?

The phosphorescent bone of a snapper
A fish within a fish

My fingers smell of fish. When you live on an
island, everything smells of fish.

You may swallow water in your sleep, but you
will not drown.

There is a surf shack, fish skeletons dry in the
window. Bones soaked
in salted rice wine in kitchen sink.
We are sleeping under mosquito

netting, sleep talkers
holding secrets
and drinking Holy water. liquid
splinters on retina are merely tears
blinding purple
shadows of a lost fortune, the ghost of
champagne.

We are sleepwalkers, exhausted, looking for a
bed, with each human transfer
unsayable pain,
reading the wound with my body,
grit caught inside the scar.
Single, raw vivid nerve endings
violent fragments buried deep in the marrow
space inside us.

All sadness smells of salt—it stings my tears now
and passes
through eyelashes, bitter like brine.

I would like to take a photograph of how we will
survive this
unhook sad from our bodies.
I would like to film tomorrow—through
dreamers' eyes.

In another dream. I see the woman standing in
Coral Sea last birthday was calligraphy paper and
something white mesh you wrapped in tissue &
pink rose petals,
a woman remembers what she wants... I am
walking back towards you.

In a dream, you are the carpet seller in the street
near the brewery, fermenting hops filtering in the
doorway. Inside, the Persian rugs stacked, dusty

fruits and animals, one magic flying-carpet on top
of the other.
You knew every weaver & intricate patterns of
dreamers & lovers.

You knew me well.
Pieces of Turkish delight wrapped in foil hidden
in my raincoat, green & sticky opiate hashish
& pink damask roses and hazelnut sugar, my
cocaine.

And when the wars in the Middle East broke out,
you sold the carpets and left the country.
You tell me you are ambassador of foreign places,
My embassy is out back, you said.
Will you come with me? you ask.

I have no refuge in the world
Other than my threshold
My head has no protection other than this
porch-way
The work of a Slave in this holy place
320 knots to the square inch.

There is another place I escape to in a dream with
you Lover, a photograph of a tea plantation
mint and lemon ice & mud crabs tied with string.

I promise to take you where no one can find us.

Our survival is mango and macadamia, all the
trees of the orchard will nourish us.
Sleep under the tile roof with me.

In photos of the old house, there are shutters
carved with wild animals, painted tigers at night.
A rare white tiger with blue eyes red in the dark,

he paces the mosaic floor.

Lost hours between ghosts we will be, the
bleeding fingers, dust, and thirst, a Persian
pattern, a prayer rug out of fractured tiles, shadow
of the artist, gluing them piece by piece onto the
verands, the ashes of afternoon sun falling on red
flowers, twisting around the wooden columns that
hold up the roof.

One pattern superimposed over the other
if you close your eyes,

you see a man and woman
through the artists eyes

one pattern superimposed over the other
fractured pieces holding together.

Can I stay here?

When he goes, the artist leaves his shadow,
In his canvas world, an island sun sets the color
of exquisite persimmons delicate grape vines
entwined, kiss his model's lips, sweet stain
magenta, wild doves in lime wood cages, the
artist leaves images after himself.
Someone walks barefoot, spilling tea, two
hundred years after we have gone.

We sleep in early afternoon under a tent of white
veils outside the curtain, mosquito sense body
heat
wild drums in the distance, of old black and white
movies, the flicker through trees.

Carry me out of tropical places to a sea house. I

miss mango tree avenue, the crocodile river with
kids on the rope swing.

If memory is a fever, let me shiver the sad years,
the hopeless ones out of my body.

Yesterday's woman picked lime buds for her bath,
then offered me a book she didn't want to read.

What gives us memory of place I asked her?

Flowers. Heat. The fever.

A woman wants a garden and a house, maybe a
dog,
two cats,
home movies, sun hat,
blue laundry sky
tanned woman wants to make love
with you
fill the cradle, pudding and milk.
We are held by ordinary things.

I will take you places where we can re-dream
our lives

There is heavy cargo inside each of us.
Written in a notebook, a map of displacement,
where the front door was, polish & beeswax.

Even the sad days—blanket bundle with dead cat.

There is a rumble of earthquake in the tropic floor
shaking the pylons anchored in the ocean bed and
a green gecko
on the tapa cloth ceiling inked brown warriors

and fighting dogs, some honey wax on the floor
in the straw roofed cottage, a baby bird stuck in
the roof wire, the mattresses were uneven but that
didn't foil conception, how ironed cotton sheets
were smooth under bare skin, and dried outside
they smell of apple blossom from the tree in the
yard and wild honey from the pollen of summer's
clover, grass candles burning.

The shape of your body dreaming
warm after sleeping in the afternoon—a stamp
embossed on soul as we enter each others borders.
Seal on my lips, tasted burnt caramel of the
ancient.

Can I see the last photograph taken of you?

She takes an image from her coat pocket.

I am a colorist, the Lover said,
soft erasure of harsh lines
on your face.

I have changed the color of your lips from pink
to red, colored flowers on your cotton dress with
ultra colors. Not soft pastels, but vibrant Pacifica
colors from my new paintbox. The photographic
paper absorbs red hibiscus and gardenias,
like litmus, the fuchsia pinks and parrot greens
like an ink blotter, you fabric is fragile as the skin
of a Chinese paper fan. Some parts tear when I
touch with sable brush
I wish you could see what I see. The change
in you makes me smile. In the transformation
you forget material pain. Look ahead and catch
yourself laughing out loud.

You've changed my blue dress to a garden.

The last picture I have of you standing in flowers.
Rain falls.
A drop on grass near your bare feet.
I paint your toes tomato red. A white rag soaks up
magenta spills. Manilla lace torn into a thousand
rags was once
the underskirt of your wedding dress.

You suit bright colors. See? How the corners of
your mouth
turn up as Mona Lisa?

A quiet dilution soothes the loss in your eyes. An
illusion of last moment captured before your
smile. Your eyelids half closed, as if filtered
through a veil.
You were standing inside a mirror looking
outwards. The morning we love, you are cloaked
in an angel veil, the photograph of you standing
in the sun; I feel
the gold of your fabric, the blanket
as you wrap around me again, the Lover said.

Tell me...what do you trust.

I trust words

I confess I fell in love with your words,
but your words made me restless.
I searched for a bleak landscape, a place with
dark soul.
that's what you said Russia was,
enter a cold space, release bindings, and go
beyond boundaries.

Tell me of the torso on page 139. I see a bronze
statue of a man, as if he has fallen leaden from a
great height, his life
flowing from a hole where his head was torn off.

It had been raining, the Lover said, while taking
my hand.
And then he seduced me, discovered my fear,
staring back at the drowned man floating on the
surface of the river. He drowned outside himself.
Then he turned frozen marble.

Tell me about the black and white photographs.
The woman walking down steps, her hair bound
in a turban. Her dress gossamer thin, her breasts,
the layout of her nipples, the forest of dark hair
below her belly. I sense a waterfall though I can't
see one.

I could tell when you embarked on this journey,
something was wrong.
I watched you shadowed by atmospheric
phantoms. A mountain dangles upside down in
the sky.
I saw red cliffs mirrored
along the wilderness of glass.

I believed in a mirage
instead of miracles.

I remember your lineament...of Arcadia
and the butterfly effect of
paper moths that sleep in wheat.
the pulse of birth and cry of carrion crow.
the milk-white fall of paper
shaken under a dome of glass
paper weight of rudimentary dreams.

Instead of feeling the cold
You taste it inside sheets of snow.

Another Angel is slaughtered at the
crossing. Her wings broken by silence.

Petals from a black rose, fall like
confetti from the signal box and
cover the angel's
shadow.

The woman in the photograph on the cover...
was she your lover, I ask.

I cannot say. I only write words to explain her.

He takes his finger and writes her world
in greasy dust of the dining car window. When
he finishes he pulls glass until it slips down
his words falling into soft erasure.

The air from Caucasus Mountains is chill through
the window the wind drags like a shroud
his voice screaming through a mountain tunnel
a train traveling three hundred miles
inside a crypt of earth.

No torture. No executions. No music.
A Man plays ivories with iron fingers; his rusty
nails scratch her name in the door, for him and
stray wolf that follows.

A chequerboard Bishop
falls between cracks
while dreams stare back
at the end of the game

some ivory pawns remain.

There are birds hatched from
enamel eggs
a knight birthed on Holy Sunday
the remains of the umbilical cord
thick rope connecting
undercarriage.

I disembark in simple places. That is all I need.
A reason to leave, a place to stop, and journey in
between...but I dreamed of a woman with green
eyes boarding the same train.

Sharing a chunk of cheese, a bottle of vodka.
He carries the bottle and holds glasses between
the knuckles of one hand.
Small glasses of spirits. Etched glass, some swans
skimming water.

We cross over bolts and shackles that hold the
dining car to the sleeping car, retreating through a
corridor to a curtained compartment.
Inside, walls covered with silk and velvet,
leather bench seats, tapestry cushions; a
chandelier, crystal drops jangling, gilt mirrors
on ceiling, grapes and pomegranate, of jeweled
and enameled eggs and doves holding verse
in gold leaf beaks; cherubs watching through
revolutionary eyes.

The Ghosts return to find the green eyed woman
and her Lover, lying primal naked, warm under
bear skin.
Windows in the East. The sun comes to light.

A wedding band worn on the finger

connects to her heart,
three colors of gold on her finger set like a puzzle.
And if she ever takes off the ring, the metal floats
apart.

Is this how we forget the fugitive years.

Each Christmas will remind us....

A Russian doll in gold tissue, I wired her on top
of the tree.

What does the doll look like?

Paper maché face, jet beads around her neck, tiny
forms like foil chocolate wrapper. Her small face
still in a smile but her forehead holds a dent now.
She is beautiful but not perfect.

Something else?

The rag was a dress you bought me
I wore it to the ocean, I floated in a lake
when I walked home late, you could see right
through me so transparent,
you counted all my bones.

And shoes with holes in the soles...

They remind me of hard luck times, like shadows
under your eyes.

You know, life goes on, pigeons shit and it falls
putty graffiti on gray concrete and there is brown
litter from paper bags
and decaying leaves, clogging the gutter.

*Lately it was your voice, like a foreign language
that makes me drift into other countries: he said.*

Without maps; the way I fell across boarders,
the old photographs of lovers, ancient passports
obsolete.

*My eyes grit now, I see red patterns shake up sky
and water tastes salt, like someone cried into my
glass.*

I almost destroyed the morning smile
the man who brings me orange juice
in a glass with
transparency of bees flying around straw
honey pot.
her juice he squeezed, not knowing
a woman's darkness, I opened my mouth.

Traces of your pollen left behind.

The man on the radio talks about the architecture
of marriage.
...who knows if it can last, he says.
He speaks of three days of rain...a play he wrote
in a drought,
Fragments together form an unbroken heart, he
said.
It is easy to break a heart:
Can we put pieces of us together? I ask.

There are more ways a heart can be broken
than a heart can stay intact.
your arm folded across my chest, heavy like the
broken wing of

an angel.

The weave of white traps your breath as heat...

Think about the architecture of love. How we
build so permanently
slowly we forget we are partners for each other.

In places you leave small findings, a briefcase full
of stones.

It was Thursday morning when my wedding ring
slipped
into the surf: he said.
Invisible to the eye, the way the tide sucks around
the rocks, it is impossible
to find a ring in the geometry of moving water,
abacus of stones, infinity of sand.

Why in this place? Why now when I have lost
everything, the Lover shouted.
I could not come back and show you more loss.

... someone help me.

You can find your ring, the Aeolian ghost spoke to
him in an ancient voice of recollections, filaments
back from vanishing point.
Her eyes drawn in black kohl pencil, the shape of
a fish.

... *a wedding ring means nothing if there is no
love*
keep searching until the gold comes back,
in the process of appearing and disappearing
you always find lost things, you are lucky that
way.

As a small boy you could glimpse it on the other

side, there is a small harp set at the entrance of
our breathing, a sixth sense, the movement is
delicate,
it starts as a sigh and moves beyond all limits,
like a ghost, is vast, you take infinity into your
lungs... say the word.

Remember when you were a small boy sailing
on a blow-up rubber mattress; she reminded him.
No one saw you leave the beach.
You sailed without rudder, without anchor,
the wind blowing.
you sailed without compass or mariners map.

no direction is true.

you sailed into the middle of the shipping lane,
by a night beacon blinking red & green.
floating, pushed by wind the boy sat.

Use your hand to ladle water from the sea, your
fingers a sieve, sifting through sand and fish
bones.
And the ring slipped back on wedding finger.

I kissed its metal.

It was some confirmation of us, when something
feels so lost. But then you find it again.

Can we say our wedding vows over? I have
ruined them with lies.

Looking back at the groom. He carries his bride
across the bridge of sighs: her veil,
ivory rice, virgin's bower, lovage strewn at her
feet.

Gather up the silk of her in his arms.

He pulls a fish hook
from her lips and kisses
a woman remembers

breaking champagne bubbles with lips
Grenache grapes
ancient vines holding bare roots.

From memory we begin again
all moments are taken like an image in a photo
pictures of each other
naked, crying, waking, swimming, laughing
that was you,
that was me, that was us.

Amber preserves a butterfly, the way we preserve
memory,
feel this,
dream this, imagine nothing is extinct. It is only
us forgetting what was . . .
in sand dunes, red tent above, he ties my fabric
with wild grass, warm dunes, Coral Sea.

Do not forget us...

I find myself falling deep
into your beautiful words again, Lover...

blurring my senses to everything

your voice magnetic
a strong pull opens up

and all that is submerged inside

breaks the surface

I drop one tear a day
while I disobey the laws of desire

forming a vast lake with a transparent skin
that reflects
a full moon

I see the dream that has grown
between the words
a crosscurrent of feelings there inside the legend

sensual and earthy
I am aware of the taboo
as the words turn alive leaving me
with sensual hunger

to suddenly touch you.

Perfumed frangipani
fell like rain over red tent
a scroll of vellum
handwritten with a feather
pure white
it was ours, long ago.

If you and I stand together on a dirt road
make one star wish....

we receive, we loose and whatever is left after the losses,
the remains of life, can we keep?

The only thing we have left that belongs to us—is us:

she whispered.

Can I ask you a question?

If a body is a star or a human being...
what are you tonight?

A tent...he answered.
...if I were a tent, would you put me up for the
night?

You know I always will.

You remember back a thousand years ago

first touch—reminds me.

In the lime trees, flocks of wild green parrots.

Their song, a sound bite shredded by winds &
desiccated waves booming on shore.
A background that softens our words to a whisper.

Looking back at the bird, hold one feather
between your fingers, the bird becomes
words migrating over paper, she whispered.

Did you write me letters a thousand years ago
Lover?

I watch you in the shadow lands before us
the black powder in a porcelain dish,
the drops of water mercurial
you mix earth and river to write me a poem

Deep sepia between strata

We are fossils sleeping on soft pillows.

But I am naked, with no pockets to hold the
poem, a map of where we are going, history of
where we have come
from.

And what secrets are left remain in my wrist
pulse
And when I die...
Stay in the bones of my spine?

Through my life lover, I am left with traces of
you,
Fragments felt in everything I touch.
I entered your room without knocking as if I
walked into a room that felt like my own.
I stayed, quietly falling in love with the man I
found there,
until I forgot how to leave.

Traveling with the same person since I was
seventeen,
carrying this feeling inside...
we never left each other.

There are scars ripped open
rusted photographs inside your eyes
watching burning roses
turn to poems
that scent my memory

the sound of a bath being filled

I open and fill with thoughts of you
laid bare for you to read.

Some diaries I burned during the fugitive years.
They were written in dead languages without a
false note.

I burned them because they remembered too
much.

Each fragment,
Living as a witness to the love between us,
I am beginning to see
an absolute confessional to my lover
as if it were the last thing written to you,
before I leave...

and if I could wish for all lovers to return to
beginnings...
kite strings turned into wishing sticks,
I would.

Look for me again Lover.

I will carry your children. A boy child on my right
hip and a girl on my left.

I will find you by your green eyes, your long hair
I will look for a girl before the woman.

She is standing in a river looking back over her
shoulder,
the Lover said.

*It is early afternoon, in May, when I find you
again...*

SUSAN BLANSHARD

Born in England, she later moved to New Zealand where she spent most of her early childhood. The daughter of a Diplomat, she had a nomadic upbringing. As a girl, she was educated in the United States and later returned to New Zealand where she had a career as an award winning senior advertising copywriter. She was sole owner and director of Mossmoon, a creative freelance agency. Her selected poetry, Fragments of The Human Heart appears in World Literary Review, Projected Letters, Volume 4, 2005.

Susan writes in different locations. Subsequently, she drew on her years living in the South Pacific. Travel writings from tropical far north Queensland, Australia; correspondence exchanged during a sojourn in South West France. Journals and poems written in French Polynesia. Sheetstone was completed during her year at Piha Beach on the West Coast of New Zealand in the South Pacific, where she returned to live for a while.

With family in the Northern and Southern Hemispheres, Susan travels between Australia, New Zealand and England. Susan lives with an artist. She has two grown-up children.

www.ingramcontent.com/pod-product-compliance
Lightning Source LLC
Chambersburg PA
CBHW030039100526
44590CB00011B/266